Ethics in Augmented Realities

A Cultural Study

Miguel Ivanov

ISBN: 9781779666260
Imprint: Press for Play Books
Copyright © 2024 Miguel Ivanov.
All Rights Reserved.

Contents

Introduction	1
The Rise of Virtual Reality Worlds	1
Chapter One: Virtual Reality and the Self	13
Understanding Identity in Virtual Reality	13
Bibliography	21
Bibliography	35
Chapter Two: Morality and Virtual Reality	41
Ethics in Virtual Worlds	41
Bibliography	67
Chapter Three: Cultural Perspectives on Virtual Reality	69
Cultural Diversity in Virtual Worlds	69
Bibliography	75
Bibliography	81
Bibliography	91
Chapter Four: Virtual Reality and Human Rights	99
Equal Access to Virtual Reality	99
Bibliography	111
Bibliography	117

Bibliography 121

Index 129

Introduction

The Rise of Virtual Reality Worlds

Exploring the Origins of Virtual Reality

The concept of Virtual Reality (VR) can be traced back to the mid-20th century, where the seeds of this immersive technology were sown in the fertile ground of science fiction and early computing. The origins of VR are a fascinating blend of technological innovation, artistic vision, and philosophical inquiry, which together laid the groundwork for the virtual experiences we encounter today.

Early Concepts and Theoretical Foundations

The term "virtual reality" itself emerged in the late 1980s, popularized by computer scientist Jaron Lanier, who co-founded VPL Research, one of the first companies to sell VR products. However, the theoretical underpinnings of VR date back much further. One of the earliest conceptual frameworks can be found in the works of American author and inventor Morton Heilig, who developed the Sensorama in the 1960s. The Sensorama was a multi-sensory experience that combined 3D visuals, sound, vibrations, and even scents to create an immersive environment for the user. Heilig's work emphasized the importance of engaging multiple senses to create a convincing illusion of reality, a principle that remains central to VR design today.

The Role of Computing Technology

The evolution of computing technology played a pivotal role in the development of VR. In the 1960s and 1970s, advancements in computer graphics and human-computer interaction began to take shape. One notable example is the work of Ivan Sutherland, who developed the first head-mounted display (HMD) system, known as the Sword of Damocles, in 1968. This rudimentary device allowed users to experience a simple virtual environment, albeit with significant limitations in terms of graphics and comfort. The Sword of Damocles highlighted both the potential and the challenges of creating immersive virtual experiences.

As computing technology progressed, so too did the capabilities of VR systems. The introduction of more powerful graphics processing units (GPUs) in the 1990s enabled the creation of more sophisticated virtual environments. This period also saw the emergence of VR gaming and entertainment, with titles like "Dactyl Nightmare" and "Virtuality" arcade games bringing VR to the public's attention. However, these early forays into VR were often limited by high costs and technological constraints, which hindered widespread adoption.

Philosophical Implications and Cultural Context

The philosophical implications of VR have been explored by various thinkers, drawing connections between virtual experiences and concepts of reality, identity, and existence. The famous thought experiment known as the "Simulation Hypothesis," proposed by philosopher Nick Bostrom, suggests that it is possible we are living in a simulated reality. This notion invites profound questions about the nature of consciousness and the distinction between the virtual and the real.

Moreover, cultural contexts have significantly influenced the development of VR. Science fiction literature and films, such as Philip K. Dick's "Do Androids Dream of Electric Sheep?" and the film "The Matrix," have shaped public perceptions of virtual worlds, often depicting them as both utopian and dystopian spaces. These narratives reflect society's hopes and fears regarding technology's impact on human experience, prompting discussions about the ethical implications of living in increasingly immersive digital environments.

Contemporary Applications and Ethical Considerations

In contemporary society, VR has found applications across various fields, including education, healthcare, and entertainment. For instance, VR simulations are used in medical training to provide realistic surgical experiences without the risks associated with real-life procedures. However, as VR technology becomes more integrated into our lives, ethical considerations surrounding its use emerge. Issues such as the potential for addiction, the blurring of reality and virtuality, and the impact on mental health must be addressed.

Furthermore, the accessibility of VR technology raises important questions about equity and inclusion. As VR systems become more affordable and user-friendly, ensuring that diverse populations can access and benefit from these technologies is crucial. This includes considering the needs of individuals with disabilities, who may require tailored VR experiences to fully engage with virtual environments.

Conclusion

In summary, the origins of virtual reality are rooted in a rich tapestry of technological advancements, philosophical inquiries, and cultural narratives. From early experiments with multi-sensory experiences to the development of sophisticated VR systems, the journey of VR reflects humanity's ongoing quest for new ways to explore and understand reality. As we continue to navigate the complexities of virtual worlds, it is essential to engage in critical discussions about the ethical implications of these technologies and their impact on our identities, relationships, and society as a whole.

$$VR = \text{Immersive Experience} + \text{User Interaction} + \text{Technological Innovation} \quad (1)$$

The Evolution of Virtual Reality Technology

The evolution of virtual reality (VR) technology is a fascinating journey that encompasses a variety of technological advancements, theoretical frameworks, and cultural shifts. The term "virtual reality" was first coined in the 1980s, but the roots of VR can be traced back much further, with significant contributions from various fields including computer science, psychology, and even art.

Early Developments

The origins of VR can be linked to the invention of the first flight simulator in the 1920s, which aimed to train pilots using rudimentary visual and auditory feedback. This early form of simulation laid the groundwork for more advanced systems. In the 1960s, Ivan Sutherland created the first head-mounted display (HMD), known as the "Sword of Damocles," which provided a primitive form of augmented reality but was limited by the technology of the time. The HMD was bulky, tethered to a computer, and required significant computational power, which was not readily available.

The 1980s and 1990s Boom

The 1980s saw a surge of interest in VR, fueled by advancements in computer graphics and interactive design. Companies like VPL Research introduced products such as the DataGlove and the EyePhone, which allowed users to interact with virtual environments using hand movements and head tracking. This period also marked the emergence of VR in entertainment, with attractions like Disney's "Aladdin's Magic Carpet Ride" and the Virtuality Group's arcade games, which offered immersive experiences to the public.

However, the excitement of the 1990s was met with challenges. The technology was still in its infancy, and issues such as low resolution, latency, and motion sickness hindered widespread adoption. The commercial failure of products like Sega's VR headset for the Genesis console exemplified the disconnect between public interest and technological capability.

The 21st Century: Resurgence and Innovation

The early 2000s witnessed a decline in VR interest, often referred to as the "VR winter." However, this period also laid the groundwork for the resurgence of VR technology in the 2010s. The advent of powerful mobile processors, advancements in display technology, and the rise of social media created an environment ripe for innovation.

In 2012, the Kickstarter campaign for the Oculus Rift marked a pivotal moment in the evolution of VR. The project garnered significant funding and attention, leading to the development of a new generation of VR headsets. This resurgence was further amplified by the introduction of other devices such as the HTC Vive and Sony's PlayStation VR, which capitalized on the growing interest in immersive gaming and experiences.

Current State of VR Technology

Today, VR technology has evolved to include sophisticated tracking systems, haptic feedback devices, and highly detailed graphics. The use of photogrammetry and 3D scanning allows for the creation of realistic virtual environments, blurring the lines between the digital and physical worlds. Furthermore, the integration of artificial intelligence (AI) into VR experiences has opened new avenues for personalized and adaptive interactions.

Despite these advancements, challenges remain. Issues such as user comfort, accessibility, and the ethical implications of virtual interactions continue to be topics of discussion among developers and researchers. The potential for addiction and escapism raises questions about the psychological effects of prolonged VR use.

Theoretical Frameworks

The evolution of VR technology is not solely a technical narrative; it is also deeply intertwined with various theoretical frameworks. The concept of presence, or the feeling of being "there" in a virtual environment, is critical to understanding user experience in VR. According to Slater and Wilbur (1997), presence can be categorized into two types: *spatial presence*, which refers to the sensation of being in a place, and *social presence*, which pertains to the awareness of others in the virtual space.

Mathematically, presence can be modeled as a function of several variables, including immersion (I), interaction (X), and realism (R):

$$P = f(I, X, R) \qquad (2)$$

Where P represents the perceived presence. This equation underscores the importance of creating immersive environments that facilitate meaningful interactions.

Examples and Future Directions

As we look to the future, the potential applications of VR technology continue to expand. Industries such as healthcare, education, and real estate are increasingly leveraging VR for training, simulations, and virtual tours. For instance, VR is being used in medical training to simulate surgeries, allowing students to practice in a risk-free environment.

Moreover, as VR technology becomes more accessible, the ethical implications surrounding its use will require careful consideration. Issues such as data privacy, consent, and the potential for virtual harassment must be addressed to ensure that the evolution of VR technology aligns with ethical standards.

In conclusion, the evolution of virtual reality technology is a complex interplay of innovation, cultural shifts, and ethical considerations. As we continue to explore the possibilities of VR, it is essential to remain mindful of the implications it holds for identity, morality, and human rights in both virtual and real-world contexts.

The Impact of Virtual Reality in Various Fields

Virtual Reality (VR) has emerged as a transformative technology across multiple domains, fundamentally altering how individuals and organizations engage with information, experiences, and each other. This section will explore the significant impacts of VR in various fields, including education, healthcare, entertainment, and social interaction, while addressing the associated theoretical frameworks, challenges, and real-world examples.

Education

The integration of VR into educational settings has revolutionized traditional teaching methodologies. By creating immersive learning environments, VR enables students to engage with content in a more interactive and experiential manner. According to [?], immersive environments can enhance learning outcomes by providing realistic simulations that facilitate active participation.

For instance, medical students can practice surgical procedures in a risk-free virtual environment, allowing for repeated practice and skill acquisition without the ethical concerns associated with real patients [?]. Similarly, history students can explore ancient civilizations through virtual reconstructions, fostering a deeper understanding of cultural contexts and historical events.

However, the implementation of VR in education also poses challenges. Accessibility remains a significant barrier, as not all students have equal access to VR technologies. Furthermore, educators must be adequately trained to integrate these tools into their curricula effectively [?].

Healthcare

In healthcare, VR is being utilized for pain management, rehabilitation, and exposure therapy. Research by [?] indicates that VR can significantly reduce pain perception during medical procedures, as patients are distracted by immersive experiences. For example, virtual environments designed for relaxation can help patients cope with anxiety and discomfort associated with treatments.

In rehabilitation, VR allows patients recovering from injuries to engage in therapeutic exercises in a controlled and motivating environment. A study by [?] demonstrated that VR-based rehabilitation programs improved motor function in stroke patients more effectively than conventional therapies.

Despite its potential, the use of VR in healthcare raises ethical concerns, particularly regarding patient consent and data privacy. Ensuring that patients are fully informed about the risks and benefits of VR treatments is crucial for maintaining ethical standards [?].

Entertainment

The entertainment industry has been one of the earliest adopters of VR technology, creating immersive experiences that captivate audiences. Video games, in particular, have seen a significant transformation with the introduction of VR headsets, allowing players to step into virtual worlds and interact with them in unprecedented ways.

The success of games like *Beat Saber* and *Half-Life: Alyx* illustrates the potential of VR to create engaging and interactive narratives. According to [?], these experiences can enhance emotional engagement and provide players with a sense of agency that traditional gaming formats cannot offer.

However, the immersive nature of VR also raises concerns about addiction and escapism. As users become more engrossed in virtual worlds, they may neglect real-life responsibilities and relationships, leading to negative consequences for their mental health and social well-being [?].

Social Interaction

VR has the potential to reshape social interactions by creating virtual spaces where individuals can connect regardless of geographical barriers. Platforms like *VRChat* and *AltspaceVR* allow users to socialize, attend events, and collaborate in immersive environments.

The concept of the *metaverse*, a collective virtual shared space, has gained traction as a new frontier for social interaction. This evolution raises questions about identity, representation, and community dynamics in virtual spaces. As [?] notes, the ability to create and manipulate avatars can lead to complex social dynamics, including issues of authenticity and discrimination.

However, the virtual nature of these interactions can also lead to challenges related to harassment and toxic behavior. Ensuring safe and inclusive environments in VR social spaces requires robust moderation and community guidelines [?].

Conclusion

The impact of virtual reality across various fields is profound, offering unique opportunities for innovation and engagement. However, alongside these benefits, it is essential to address the ethical considerations and challenges that arise from its use. As VR technology continues to evolve, ongoing research and dialogue will be crucial in navigating its implications for society.

The Need for Ethical Considerations in Virtual Reality

The advent of virtual reality (VR) has transformed the way individuals interact with digital environments, providing immersive experiences that can significantly alter perceptions, behaviors, and social dynamics. As these technologies continue to evolve, the necessity for ethical considerations becomes increasingly pressing. This section will explore the implications of VR on ethics, highlighting the critical need for a robust framework to address the unique challenges presented by this medium.

The Unique Nature of Virtual Reality

Virtual reality is distinct from traditional media due to its immersive and interactive nature. Unlike watching a film or reading a book, VR places users inside a three-dimensional environment where they can engage with digital entities and manipulate their surroundings. This level of immersion can lead to a profound sense of presence and emotional engagement, which raises ethical questions regarding user experience and the responsibilities of developers.

Psychological Impact of Immersion

One of the primary ethical concerns in VR is its psychological impact on users. Research indicates that the immersive nature of VR can lead to a phenomenon known as the "Proteus Effect," where individuals change their behavior in the real world based on their virtual avatars' characteristics. For example, a user who embodies a confident, attractive avatar may exhibit increased self-esteem and assertiveness in real life. Conversely, negative experiences in VR, such as harassment or violence, can lead to desensitization or increased aggression in the real world.

$$\text{Behavior Change} = f(\text{Avatar Characteristics}, \text{User Experience}) \qquad (3)$$

This equation suggests that the behavior change of a user is a function of the avatar's characteristics and the overall user experience within the virtual environment. Consequently, developers must consider the implications of avatar design and user interactions, ensuring that they promote positive psychological outcomes while mitigating harmful effects.

Ethical Design Principles

To address these concerns, ethical design principles must be integrated into the development of VR experiences. This includes ensuring user consent, transparency, and the right to disengage from potentially harmful situations. For instance, developers should provide clear information about the nature of the VR experience and any potential risks involved. Additionally, mechanisms for users to report harassment or abuse should be easily accessible, promoting a safe environment for all participants.

The Role of Virtual Law

As virtual environments gain popularity, the question of governance arises. The emergence of virtual law—rules and regulations tailored to govern behavior in digital spaces—highlights the need for ethical standards that can be enforced within VR. This includes defining acceptable behavior, establishing consequences for violations, and ensuring that virtual communities foster inclusivity and respect.

Cultural Sensitivity and Representation

Moreover, the ethical implications of cultural representation in virtual worlds cannot be overlooked. The risk of cultural appropriation and misrepresentation poses significant challenges. Developers must strive for cultural sensitivity, ensuring that diverse perspectives are accurately represented and respected. This can involve collaborating with cultural experts and community members during the design process to create authentic and respectful virtual experiences.

Case Studies and Examples

Several case studies illustrate the importance of ethical considerations in VR. For instance, the game *Second Life* faced criticism for allowing users to create and engage in content that perpetuated stereotypes and facilitated harassment. In response, developers implemented community guidelines and moderation tools to promote a safer environment. Similarly, the VR experience *Tilt Brush* faced backlash over the lack of accessibility features for users with disabilities, prompting a reevaluation of inclusivity in design.

Conclusion

In conclusion, the need for ethical considerations in virtual reality is paramount as the technology continues to evolve and permeate various aspects of society. By prioritizing ethical design principles, promoting cultural sensitivity, and establishing virtual laws, developers can create immersive experiences that not only entertain but also respect and empower users. As we navigate this new frontier, it is essential to foster an ethical framework that addresses the unique challenges posed by virtual realities, ensuring that they contribute positively to the human experience rather than detract from it.

The Purpose and Scope of the Cultural Study

The advent of virtual reality (VR) has revolutionized the way we interact with digital environments, prompting a critical examination of the ethical implications that accompany these immersive experiences. This cultural study aims to investigate the multifaceted relationship between virtual reality and ethical considerations, focusing on how these technologies shape, reflect, and challenge our understanding of identity, morality, culture, and human rights.

Purpose of the Study

The primary purpose of this study is to explore the ethical dimensions of virtual reality as a cultural phenomenon. As VR technology continues to evolve, it becomes increasingly important to address the ethical dilemmas that arise within these digital spaces. This study seeks to:

- Analyze the impact of virtual reality on individual identity and self-perception, highlighting the potential for both positive and negative outcomes.

- Investigate the moral responsibilities of users and developers within virtual environments, including the implications of virtual actions on real-world behavior.

- Examine cultural diversity and representation in virtual worlds, emphasizing the need for ethical considerations in the design and implementation of VR experiences.

- Address human rights issues related to access, privacy, and discrimination in virtual reality, advocating for inclusivity and fairness in these digital realms.

By articulating these objectives, the study aims to contribute to a deeper understanding of the ethical landscape of virtual reality and to foster discussions that encourage responsible practices among developers, users, and policymakers.

Scope of the Study

This cultural study will encompass a broad range of topics related to ethics in virtual reality, organized into four key areas: identity, morality, cultural perspectives, and human rights. Each area will be explored through a combination of theoretical frameworks, empirical research, and case studies. The following outlines the scope of each section:

1. **Identity in Virtual Reality:** This section will delve into the concept of the digital self, examining how virtual avatars serve as extensions of identity and the psychological impact of virtual experiences on personal authenticity. It will also address the challenges of privacy and body image issues, alongside the potential for identity manipulation within virtual spaces.

2. **Morality in Virtual Reality:** Here, the study will explore the emergence of ethical systems within virtual worlds, discussing the moral responsibilities of users and the role of virtual law in governing behavior. The implications of immersive storytelling and the capacity of VR to cultivate empathy will also be evaluated, alongside the ethical dilemmas posed by morally grey choices.

3. **Cultural Perspectives:** This section will focus on cultural representation in virtual environments, analyzing the impact of cultural biases and the importance of preserving cultural heritage. The study will also investigate issues of cultural appropriation and the potential for virtual reality to facilitate intercultural communication and understanding.

4. **Human Rights in Virtual Reality:** The final section will address the digital divide and the importance of accessibility for marginalized groups, including people with disabilities. Topics such as privacy rights, freedom of speech, and the right to disconnect will be examined, emphasizing the need for ethical considerations in promoting inclusivity and diversity within virtual spaces.

Methodological Approach

To achieve the objectives outlined above, this study will employ a mixed-methods approach, combining qualitative and quantitative research methodologies. This will include:

- **Literature Review:** A comprehensive review of existing literature on virtual reality and ethics will be conducted to identify gaps in knowledge and to inform the study's theoretical framework.

- **Surveys and Interviews:** Data will be collected through surveys and interviews with VR users, developers, and ethicists to gather insights on personal experiences and ethical considerations in virtual environments.

- **Case Studies:** Selected case studies of virtual reality applications will be analyzed to illustrate the ethical challenges and successes encountered in real-world scenarios.

Significance of the Study

The significance of this cultural study lies in its potential to inform the development of ethical guidelines and best practices for virtual reality technologies. By addressing the ethical implications of virtual experiences, the study aims to promote a more responsible and inclusive approach to the design and use of VR. Furthermore, it seeks to engage stakeholders—developers, users, and policymakers—in meaningful discussions about the ethical responsibilities inherent in creating and navigating virtual worlds.

In conclusion, as virtual reality continues to shape our cultural landscape, it is imperative to critically examine the ethical dimensions of these technologies. This cultural study endeavors to illuminate the complex interplay between virtual reality and ethics, ultimately contributing to a more nuanced understanding of the impact of virtual experiences on individuals and society as a whole.

Chapter One: Virtual Reality and the Self

Understanding Identity in Virtual Reality

The Concept of the Digital Self

The notion of the **Digital Self** refers to the identity and persona that individuals construct and inhabit within virtual environments. This concept is increasingly relevant as technology evolves, allowing users to create avatars, engage in virtual interactions, and express themselves in ways that may differ significantly from their real-world identities. To understand the Digital Self, we must explore several theoretical frameworks, challenges, and examples that illustrate its complexities.

Theoretical Frameworks

The Digital Self can be analyzed through various theoretical lenses, including *social identity theory, self-presentation theory,* and *theories of embodiment.*

Social Identity Theory Social identity theory posits that individuals derive a sense of self from their group memberships. In virtual environments, users often align themselves with specific communities, which can influence their digital identities. For instance, a player in a multiplayer online game may adopt characteristics that reflect the norms and values of their chosen faction, thereby shaping their Digital Self based on social affiliations.

Self-Presentation Theory Self-presentation theory suggests that individuals actively manage their identities in social contexts to create desired impressions. In virtual spaces, users can curate their Digital Selves through avatar customization, choice of usernames, and the content they share. This curation can lead to discrepancies between a person's real-world self and their digital persona, raising questions about authenticity and representation.

Theories of Embodiment Theories of embodiment focus on how individuals experience their identities through physical and virtual bodies. In virtual reality, the sense of presence—where users feel as if they are truly inhabiting their avatars—can significantly impact their Digital Self. This embodiment can lead to heightened emotional responses and altered perceptions of self, as users may engage with their avatars in ways that reflect or challenge their real-world identities.

Challenges of the Digital Self

While the Digital Self offers opportunities for expression and exploration, it also presents several challenges:

Authenticity and Representation One of the primary concerns surrounding the Digital Self is the authenticity of virtual identities. Users may create avatars that are idealized versions of themselves or entirely different personas. This dissonance can lead to existential questions about who they truly are. For example, a user may present a confident and charismatic avatar in a virtual world while struggling with social anxiety in real life. This gap can create a sense of fragmentation in identity.

Privacy and Surveillance The Digital Self is often subject to privacy concerns, particularly regarding data collection and surveillance. Virtual environments frequently track user interactions, preferences, and behaviors, leading to potential exploitation of personal information. For instance, a user may unknowingly share sensitive information through their digital interactions, compromising their privacy and autonomy.

Identity Manipulation The potential for identity manipulation in virtual spaces raises ethical questions. Users may encounter scenarios where they can adopt identities that do not belong to them, leading to issues of cultural appropriation and misrepresentation. For example, a user may create an avatar that embodies a cultural identity different from their own, which can perpetuate stereotypes and diminish the authenticity of marginalized cultures.

Examples of the Digital Self in Practice

Several platforms and applications exemplify the concept of the Digital Self, showcasing both its potential and pitfalls:

Social Media On platforms like Instagram and TikTok, users curate their Digital Selves through carefully selected images, posts, and interactions. The pressure to maintain an idealized online persona can lead to mental health challenges, as users compare themselves to the often unrealistic standards set by others. The phenomenon of "Instagrammable" moments illustrates how the Digital Self is influenced by societal expectations and the desire for validation.

Online Gaming In gaming environments, players often create avatars that reflect their aspirations or fantasies. For instance, in games like *World of Warcraft*, players can assume roles that allow them to explore aspects of their identity that may be suppressed in real life. However, this can also lead to issues of addiction and escapism, as players may prioritize their digital lives over real-world responsibilities and relationships.

Virtual Reality Experiences Virtual reality platforms, such as *VRChat*, provide immersive experiences where users can interact with others through their avatars in real-time. The embodiment in these environments can lead to profound experiences of connection and empathy, but it can also exacerbate issues of harassment and discrimination, as users may feel emboldened to act in ways they would not in face-to-face interactions.

Conclusion

The Digital Self represents a complex interplay of identity, technology, and ethics. As individuals navigate virtual environments, they are challenged to consider the implications of their digital identities, including authenticity, privacy, and the potential for manipulation. Understanding the Digital Self is crucial for fostering healthy virtual communities and promoting ethical engagement in augmented realities. By critically examining these aspects, we can better appreciate the transformative potential of virtual spaces while addressing the ethical considerations that arise in their use.

Virtual Avatars and Personal Expression

Virtual avatars serve as digital representations of users within virtual reality (VR) environments, enabling them to navigate, interact, and express themselves in ways that may not be possible in the physical world. This section delves into the significance of avatars in personal expression, examining the interplay between identity, creativity, and the ethical implications of avatar design and usage.

The Role of Avatars in Identity Formation

Avatars are more than mere digital stand-ins; they are integral to how individuals perceive themselves and are perceived by others in virtual spaces. The concept of the *digital self* emerges from the interaction between the user and their avatar. According to [?], the digital self allows users to explore facets of their identity that may be constrained by societal norms in the physical world.

$$I_{\text{digital}} = f(A, C, E) \qquad (4)$$

where I_{digital} is the digital identity, A represents avatar attributes, C denotes cultural context, and E signifies emotional engagement.

This equation illustrates that the digital self is shaped by the characteristics of the avatar, the cultural background of the user, and their emotional experiences within the virtual environment.

Avatars as Tools for Self-Expression

The customization of avatars allows users to reflect their personality, interests, and aspirations. Users can choose physical attributes, clothing, and accessories that resonate with their self-image or desired persona. For instance, a user may create a muscular avatar to project confidence or a fantastical creature to embody creativity. This customization is supported by theories of *symbolic interactionism*, which posits that individuals derive meaning from their interactions with others and their environment [?].

However, the freedom of expression through avatars also raises ethical questions. The potential for *identity manipulation* can lead to issues such as misrepresentation and deception. In online gaming, for example, players may adopt avatars that do not reflect their real-life identities, leading to a disconnect between their virtual and physical selves.

The Psychological Impact of Avatars

The psychological effects of avatar representation are profound. Research indicates that avatars can influence users' behaviors and attitudes, a phenomenon known as the *Proteus effect* [?]. This effect suggests that individuals may adopt the characteristics of their avatars, impacting their self-esteem and social interactions. For example, a study found that users of attractive avatars exhibited higher levels of confidence in social interactions compared to those using less appealing avatars.

$$B = g(A, P) \tag{5}$$

where B represents behavior, A is the avatar's attributes, and P denotes the user's personality traits.

This relationship suggests that the design and attributes of an avatar can significantly influence user behavior in virtual environments.

Challenges of Personal Expression through Avatars

Despite the benefits of avatar-based self-expression, challenges persist. Issues of *body image* and *representation* are prevalent, particularly for marginalized groups. Avatars often reflect societal beauty standards, which can lead to negative self-perception among users who do not conform to these ideals. Furthermore, the predominance of certain body types and ethnic representations in popular VR platforms can perpetuate stereotypes and limit the diversity of avatar options available to users.

The ethical implications of avatar design extend to the responsibility of developers to create inclusive and diverse options. This is particularly crucial in fostering a sense of belonging and acceptance among users from various backgrounds.

Examples of Avatar Customization and Expression

Numerous platforms exemplify the role of avatars in personal expression. For instance, in *Second Life*, users have extensive freedom to customize their avatars, leading to a vibrant community where individuals can explore different identities. Similarly, in *VRChat*, users can create and share avatars that reflect their creativity, from realistic human representations to fantastical creatures.

However, these platforms also face challenges, such as the prevalence of harassment and discrimination based on avatar appearance. The ethical responsibility falls on both users and developers to cultivate a respectful environment where personal expression is celebrated rather than ridiculed.

Conclusion

In conclusion, virtual avatars play a pivotal role in personal expression within virtual reality. They allow users to explore and express their identities in unique ways, but this freedom is accompanied by ethical considerations surrounding representation, body image, and the psychological effects of avatar interactions. As virtual reality continues to evolve, fostering an inclusive and respectful environment for avatar customization will be essential in ensuring that personal expression thrives without compromising individual dignity or societal values.

The Influence of Virtual Experiences on Real-Life Behavior

The intersection of virtual reality (VR) and real-life behavior is a burgeoning area of interest in both psychological and sociological research. As individuals engage in immersive virtual environments, the experiences they encounter can significantly shape their attitudes, beliefs, and behaviors in the real world. This section delves into the mechanisms through which virtual experiences influence real-life behavior, drawing on relevant theories, empirical studies, and real-world examples.

Theoretical Framework

One of the foundational theories that explain the influence of virtual experiences on real-life behavior is the **Social Cognitive Theory** (Bandura, 1986). This theory posits that individuals learn and adopt new behaviors through observation and imitation of others, particularly in social contexts. In virtual environments, users often observe avatars engaging in various behaviors, which can lead to modeling effects. For instance, a player who witnesses an avatar demonstrating prosocial behavior, such as cooperation or altruism, may be more likely to replicate these behaviors in their real-life interactions.

Another relevant framework is the **Theory of Planned Behavior** (Ajzen, 1991), which suggests that an individual's intention to engage in a behavior is influenced by their attitudes, subjective norms, and perceived behavioral control. Virtual experiences can alter these components by providing users with new perspectives and experiences that shape their attitudes toward certain behaviors. For example, a VR simulation that allows users to experience the challenges faced by marginalized groups may foster empathy and lead to more supportive behaviors in real life.

Empirical Evidence

Numerous studies have examined the impact of virtual experiences on real-life behavior. One notable study by *Bailenson et al.* (2008) demonstrated that participants who embodied an avatar that was taller and more attractive exhibited increased confidence and assertiveness in subsequent real-world interactions. This phenomenon, known as **embodiment**, suggests that the physical characteristics and experiences of avatars can translate into real-world behavior changes.

Moreover, a study conducted by *Rosenberg et al.* (2013) found that participants who engaged in a VR environment simulating a climate change scenario exhibited increased environmental concern and were more likely to engage in pro-environmental behaviors, such as recycling and conservation efforts, after the experience. This indicates that immersive virtual experiences can effectively alter attitudes and behaviors toward pressing global issues.

Challenges and Ethical Considerations

Despite the potential for positive behavioral influence, there are also challenges and ethical considerations associated with the impact of virtual experiences on real-life behavior. One concern is the potential for desensitization to violence. Research by *Fowler et al.* (2015) suggests that repeated exposure to violent virtual experiences may lead to a decrease in empathy and an increase in aggressive behaviors in real-life situations. This raises important questions about the ethical implications of designing and promoting violent virtual content.

Furthermore, the **Proteus Effect** (Yee & Bailenson, 2007) highlights how the characteristics of avatars can influence user behavior. Users who embody avatars that are perceived as more powerful or attractive may engage in riskier or more aggressive behaviors, which could have negative consequences in their real-life interactions. This effect underscores the need for careful consideration of avatar design and the potential behavioral implications.

Real-World Examples

Real-world applications of VR technology have shown promising results in influencing behavior. For instance, VR has been utilized in therapeutic settings to help individuals confront phobias and anxiety disorders. A study by *Hofmann et al.* (2012) demonstrated that participants who underwent VR exposure therapy for social anxiety reported significant reductions in anxiety and increased social engagement in real-life situations.

Additionally, VR has been employed in educational contexts to enhance learning outcomes and behavior change. Programs that immerse students in historical events or scientific phenomena have been shown to increase engagement and motivation, leading to improved academic performance and real-world applications of knowledge.

Conclusion

The influence of virtual experiences on real-life behavior is a complex interplay of cognitive, emotional, and social factors. As virtual reality continues to evolve, understanding these influences will be crucial for harnessing the potential of VR for positive behavioral change while mitigating the risks associated with negative influences. Future research should focus on longitudinal studies to assess the long-term effects of virtual experiences on behavior and the ethical implications of VR content creation.

Bibliography

[1] Bandura, A. (1986). *Social foundations of thought and action: A social cognitive theory*. Englewood Cliffs, NJ: Prentice-Hall.

[2] Ajzen, I. (1991). The theory of planned behavior. *Organizational Behavior and Human Decision Processes*, 50(2), 179-211.

[3] Bailenson, J. N., Beall, A. C., Blascovich, J., & Loomis, J. M. (2008). Avatars in social media: Balancing accuracy, playfulness and embodied messages. *Computers in Human Behavior*, 24(6), 2465-2470.

[4] Rosenberg, M., & et al. (2013). The impact of virtual reality on environmental behavior. *Journal of Environmental Psychology*, 35, 1-10.

[5] Fowler, J. H., & Christakis, N. A. (2015). Cooperative behavior cascades in human social networks. *Proceedings of the National Academy of Sciences*, 107(12), 5334-5338.

[6] Yee, N., & Bailenson, J. N. (2007). The Proteus effect: The effect of transformed self-representation on behavior. *Human Communication Research*, 33(3), 271-290.

[7] Hofmann, S. G., & et al. (2012). The Efficacy of Cognitive Behavioral Therapy: A Review of Meta-analyses. *Cognitive Therapy and Research*, 36(5), 427-440.

Exploring the Notion of Authenticity in Virtual Reality

The concept of authenticity in virtual reality (VR) is a multifaceted and often contentious topic that raises important questions about identity, representation, and the nature of experience in digital environments. As users navigate these immersive worlds, they are confronted with the challenge of reconciling their digital personas with their real-life identities. This section explores various dimensions of authenticity in VR, including the implications of avatar creation, the impact of social interactions, and the philosophical underpinnings of what it means to be "authentic" in a virtual context.

Theoretical Framework

To understand authenticity in VR, we can draw from several theoretical frameworks. One relevant perspective is the **Social Identity Theory**, which posits that individuals derive a sense of self from their group memberships and social interactions. In VR, users can create avatars that may or may not reflect their real-world identities, leading to a complex interplay between personal expression and social perception.

Another pertinent framework is **Erving Goffman's Dramaturgical Theory**, which suggests that individuals perform various roles in different social contexts. In the context of VR, users may adopt exaggerated or entirely different personas, challenging traditional notions of authenticity. This leads us to question whether an avatar can ever truly represent the individual behind it, and if so, how this representation is perceived by others within the virtual space.

Challenges to Authenticity

One of the primary challenges to authenticity in VR is the phenomenon of **avatar dissonance**, where a user's avatar does not align with their real-world identity or self-perception. This dissonance can lead to feelings of alienation or inauthenticity, as users may struggle to connect their virtual experiences with their actual lives. For instance, a user who creates a powerful, idealized avatar may experience a disconnect when returning to their real-life self, potentially leading to issues related to self-esteem and body image.

Moreover, the **illusion of presence** in VR can further complicate the notion of authenticity. Users often report feeling as though they are truly "there" in the virtual environment, which can blur the lines between real and virtual experiences. This raises ethical questions about the impact of these experiences on users' perceptions of reality and their behavior in the real world. For example, a user who engages in violent behavior in a virtual space may find it difficult to reconcile that behavior with their real-life moral compass, leading to potential desensitization to violence.

Philosophical Perspectives

From a philosophical standpoint, the question of authenticity in VR can be examined through the lens of **existentialism**. Existentialist thinkers like Jean-Paul Sartre emphasize the importance of individual freedom and the responsibility that comes with it. In VR, users are afforded the freedom to create and inhabit identities that may diverge significantly from their real selves. However, this freedom also comes with the responsibility to navigate the ethical implications of their virtual actions and representations.

Furthermore, the **Simulacra and Simulation** theory by Jean Baudrillard posits that in a postmodern world, representations can become more real than reality itself. In VR, the hyperreality created by digital environments can challenge users' perceptions of authenticity, leading them to question whether their experiences are genuine or merely simulations of reality. This philosophical inquiry invites users to reflect on the value they place on authenticity within their virtual interactions.

Examples of Authenticity in Virtual Reality

Consider the popular VR platform **VRChat**, where users create avatars ranging from realistic representations of themselves to fantastical creatures. The diversity of avatars highlights the spectrum of authenticity, as some users choose to embody their true selves, while others opt for exaggerated or entirely fictional representations. This choice can lead to varied social dynamics, where users may find acceptance or rejection based on their avatar's appearance.

Another example is the rise of **virtual reality therapy**, where individuals confront their fears or traumas in controlled virtual environments. The authenticity of the therapeutic experience relies heavily on the user's ability to engage with their avatar and the virtual world genuinely. If a user feels that their avatar does not represent their true self, the effectiveness of the therapy may be compromised, highlighting the critical role of authenticity in therapeutic settings.

Conclusion

In summary, the notion of authenticity in virtual reality is a complex interplay of identity, representation, and experience. As users navigate these immersive environments, they must confront the challenges of avatar dissonance, the illusion of presence, and the philosophical implications of their virtual identities. By examining these dimensions, we can better understand the impact of VR on personal authenticity and the ethical considerations that arise from our interactions within these digital worlds. As the technology continues to evolve, so too will our understanding of what it means to be authentic in a space where the lines between real and virtual are increasingly blurred.

Challenges to Personal Privacy in Virtual Environments

As virtual reality (VR) technologies become increasingly integrated into our daily lives, the challenges to personal privacy within these environments have emerged as a critical concern. The immersive nature of VR creates a unique set of circumstances that can compromise user privacy, raising ethical questions about data collection, surveillance, and the potential for identity theft. This section explores the complexities surrounding personal privacy in virtual environments, emphasizing theoretical frameworks, real-world implications, and illustrative examples.

Theoretical Frameworks

The discourse on privacy in virtual environments can be examined through the lens of several theoretical frameworks:

- **Contextual Integrity:** This theory posits that privacy is maintained when information flows are appropriate to the context in which they are shared. In VR, the immersive experience often blurs these contextual boundaries, leading to potential breaches of privacy.

- **Surveillance Capitalism:** Coined by Shoshana Zuboff, this concept describes how personal data is commodified in digital environments. In VR, user interactions can be tracked and monetized, raising ethical concerns about consent and user agency.

- **Social Construction of Technology (SCOT):** This framework asserts that technology is shaped by social practices and norms. In VR, the design of environments can either protect or expose user privacy, depending on the values and ethics of the developers.

Data Collection and User Tracking

One of the most significant challenges to personal privacy in virtual environments is the extensive data collection that occurs during user interactions. VR systems often require a vast amount of personal data to create tailored experiences, including:

- Biometric data (e.g., eye movement, facial expressions)

- Behavioral data (e.g., user movements, interactions with virtual objects)

- Demographic data (e.g., age, gender, location)

The aggregation of this data can lead to detailed profiles of users, which can be exploited for targeted advertising, behavioral manipulation, or even unauthorized surveillance. For instance, a VR gaming platform may track a user's in-game behavior and preferences, selling that data to third-party advertisers without explicit consent.

Surveillance and Monitoring

The immersive nature of VR can create environments where users feel constantly monitored. The integration of cameras and sensors in VR headsets and environments can lead to a sense of surveillance, which may deter users from fully engaging with the experience. This is particularly concerning in social VR platforms, where interactions can be recorded and analyzed.

Consider the case of a popular social VR platform that allows users to interact in virtual spaces. If users are aware that their conversations and movements are being recorded, they may self-censor, altering their behavior and undermining the authenticity of their interactions. This phenomenon raises questions about the ethical implications of surveillance in virtual environments and the potential for creating a culture of fear and mistrust.

Identity Theft and Misrepresentation

Another pressing challenge to personal privacy in virtual environments is the risk of identity theft and misrepresentation. The creation of avatars allows users to express themselves freely, but it also opens the door for malicious actors to exploit these identities. For instance, a user may create an avatar that closely resembles another individual, leading to potential harassment or defamation.

Moreover, the anonymity provided by VR can embolden users to engage in harmful behaviors, such as cyberbullying or harassment. The case of a VR platform where users were able to create avatars that mimicked real people without their consent highlights the urgent need for identity verification and protection mechanisms in virtual environments.

Privacy by Design

To mitigate the challenges to personal privacy in virtual environments, the principle of "privacy by design" should be adopted by developers and designers. This approach emphasizes the integration of privacy considerations into the design process from the outset, rather than as an afterthought. Key strategies include:

- Implementing robust data encryption to protect user information.

- Providing users with clear and transparent privacy policies that outline data collection practices.

- Allowing users to control their data, including options to opt-out of data collection or delete their information.

By prioritizing user privacy in the design of virtual environments, developers can foster trust and encourage more meaningful engagement.

Conclusion

The challenges to personal privacy in virtual environments are multifaceted and require a nuanced understanding of the ethical implications involved. As VR technology continues to evolve, it is imperative that developers, users, and policymakers collaborate to establish frameworks that protect personal privacy while promoting innovation and creativity. Addressing these challenges will not only enhance user experience but also contribute to the responsible development of virtual reality technologies.

$$P_{privacy} = f(D_{collection}, S_{monitoring}, I_{theft}, C_{design}) \qquad (6)$$

Where:

- $P_{privacy}$ = Level of personal privacy

- $D_{collection}$ = Degree of data collection

- $S_{monitoring}$ = Extent of surveillance and monitoring

- I_{theft} = Risk of identity theft

- C_{design} = Effectiveness of privacy by design measures

Ultimately, the success of virtual reality as a transformative medium hinges on our ability to navigate these privacy challenges thoughtfully and ethically.

Virtual Reality and Body Image Issues

The advent of Virtual Reality (VR) has introduced new dimensions to the concept of body image, a psychological construct that reflects how individuals perceive their physical selves. In the immersive environments of VR, users can create and manipulate avatars that may or may not resemble their real-world bodies. This phenomenon raises critical questions about the implications of virtual body representation on self-esteem, body satisfaction, and overall psychological well-being.

Theoretical Framework

Body image is often conceptualized within the framework of social comparison theory, which posits that individuals determine their self-worth by comparing themselves to others. In VR, where users can curate their avatars to embody idealized physical traits, the potential for negative body image is heightened. According to [?], the tendency to compare oneself to others can lead to feelings of inadequacy, particularly when individuals encounter avatars that conform to societal beauty standards.

Problems Associated with Body Image in VR

The problems associated with body image in virtual environments can be categorized into several key issues:

- **Idealized Avatars:** Users often create avatars that reflect their ideal selves, which may lead to dissatisfaction with their real bodies. This phenomenon is particularly prevalent among adolescents and young adults, who are susceptible to external pressures regarding appearance.

- **Discrepancy Between Virtual and Real Bodies:** The stark contrast between an individual's avatar and their physical self can exacerbate feelings of body dissatisfaction. Research has shown that individuals who engage in VR experiences with highly idealized avatars report lower body satisfaction in real life [?].

- **Hyper-Reality of Beauty Standards:** VR can amplify unrealistic beauty standards by providing users with access to environments where only idealized bodies are represented. This hyper-reality can distort perceptions of what is normal and attainable in the real world.

- **Social Interaction and Body Image:** In social VR experiences, users often interact with others through their avatars. This interaction can lead to body image issues if individuals feel judged or compared based on their virtual representations, leading to anxiety and social withdrawal [?].

Examples of Body Image Issues in VR

Several studies highlight the impact of VR on body image:

1. **Study on Avatar Customization:** A study conducted by [?] found that participants who customized avatars to reflect more attractive features reported increased body dissatisfaction after the experience. The participants expressed feelings of inadequacy when comparing their real bodies to their virtual representations.

2. **Impact of VR Gaming:** Research by [?] indicated that players of VR games with customizable characters often experienced a decline in body image satisfaction, particularly when their avatars were significantly more muscular or slim than their actual bodies.

3. **Women and Body Image:** A study focusing on female users of VR platforms revealed that women who engaged in environments that emphasized beauty and body aesthetics reported heightened levels of body shame and dissatisfaction. This finding suggests that the context of VR experiences plays a crucial role in shaping body image perceptions [?].

Ethical Considerations

Given the profound implications of VR on body image, several ethical considerations emerge:

- **Responsibility of Developers:** VR developers have a responsibility to create environments that promote positive body image. This includes offering diverse avatar options that reflect a range of body types, ethnicities, and ages, thereby fostering inclusivity and acceptance.

- **User Education:** Educating users about the potential impacts of VR on body image is crucial. Awareness campaigns can help users navigate the complexities of virtual self-representation and mitigate negative psychological effects.

- **Regulating Content:** There should be regulatory frameworks in place to monitor and manage content that promotes harmful body standards. This includes scrutinizing advertising and promotional materials within VR platforms that may perpetuate unrealistic beauty ideals.

Conclusion

In conclusion, the intersection of Virtual Reality and body image presents significant challenges and opportunities. While VR can serve as a tool for self-exploration and empowerment, it also has the potential to exacerbate body dissatisfaction and contribute to negative self-perceptions. As VR technology continues to evolve, it is imperative that stakeholders—developers, users, and researchers—collaborate to foster environments that promote healthy body image and psychological well-being. The ethical implications of body representation in VR must be at the forefront of discussions surrounding the future of virtual environments.

The Potential for Identity Manipulation in Virtual Reality

The advent of virtual reality (VR) has opened up unprecedented avenues for self-expression and identity exploration. However, alongside these opportunities lies a significant potential for identity manipulation, raising ethical questions about the authenticity of experiences and the psychological impacts on users. This section delves into the complexities surrounding identity manipulation in VR, examining the theoretical frameworks, associated problems, and illustrative examples.

Theoretical Frameworks

Identity manipulation in virtual reality can be understood through various theoretical lenses, including social identity theory, symbolic interactionism, and postmodern identity theory.

Social Identity Theory Social identity theory posits that individuals derive a sense of self from their group memberships. In virtual environments, users can adopt multiple avatars, each representing different facets of their identity. This multiplicity allows for the exploration of various social identities, but it also raises concerns about the fragmentation of the self. As users oscillate between these identities, they may experience cognitive dissonance, leading to confusion about their real-world identity.

Symbolic Interactionism Symbolic interactionism emphasizes the role of social interactions in shaping identity. In VR, the interactions between avatars can significantly influence users' self-perception. For instance, a user who adopts a powerful avatar may experience an increase in confidence, altering their real-world behavior. However, this manipulation can lead to an exaggerated sense of self, where users may struggle to reconcile their virtual experiences with their actual lives.

Postmodern Identity Theory Postmodern identity theory suggests that identity is fluid and constructed through experiences and interactions. In VR, users can curate their identities by selecting avatars, costumes, and behaviors. While this offers a liberating space for self-exploration, it also raises ethical questions about authenticity and the potential for misrepresentation. The ability to manipulate one's identity can lead to deceptive practices, complicating the nature of interpersonal relationships in both virtual and real-life contexts.

Problems Associated with Identity Manipulation

While the ability to manipulate identity in VR offers exciting possibilities, it also presents several problems:

Authenticity and Deception One of the primary concerns regarding identity manipulation is the issue of authenticity. Users may present idealized versions of themselves, leading to a disconnect between their virtual and real-world identities. This can result in deceptive interactions, where individuals engage with avatars that do not accurately represent the person behind the screen. Such deception can erode trust in virtual communities and complicate interpersonal relationships.

Psychological Impact The psychological impact of identity manipulation can be profound. Users who immerse themselves in alternate identities may experience a blurring of boundaries between their virtual and real selves. This can lead to identity crises, anxiety, or even depression, especially for those who struggle to reconcile their virtual experiences with their real-world identities. The phenomenon of "avatar identification," where users become emotionally attached to their avatars, can exacerbate these issues.

Exploitation and Harassment Identity manipulation can also facilitate exploitation and harassment. Users may create avatars that embody harmful stereotypes or engage in predatory behavior, taking advantage of the anonymity provided by virtual environments. This manipulation of identity can lead to harassment, discrimination, and a toxic atmosphere within virtual spaces, raising ethical concerns about user safety and well-being.

Examples of Identity Manipulation in VR

To illustrate the potential for identity manipulation in virtual reality, consider the following examples:

Gaming Avatars   In many online multiplayer games, players create avatars that can be drastically different from their real selves. For instance, a user may choose to embody a powerful warrior or a mythical creature, allowing them to explore aspects of identity that may be suppressed in their real life. While this can be empowering, it may also lead to an inflated sense of self-worth or, conversely, feelings of inadequacy when comparing oneself to the idealized avatars of others.

Social VR Platforms   Platforms like VRChat and Second Life enable users to create and customize their avatars extensively. Users can adopt identities that reflect their fantasies or aspirations, leading to a rich tapestry of self-expression. However, this can also result in scenarios where users misrepresent themselves, leading to relationships built on false pretenses. For example, a user may present themselves as a different gender or age, complicating the dynamics of social interactions and trust.

Therapeutic Applications   In therapeutic settings, VR is being used to help individuals explore and confront aspects of their identity. However, this manipulation of identity can be a double-edged sword. While it offers a safe space for exploration, it can also lead to the reinforcement of negative self-perceptions if users engage with avatars that embody their insecurities. For instance, a user struggling with body image issues may create an avatar that exaggerates their perceived flaws, perpetuating a cycle of negative self-talk.

Ethical Considerations

The potential for identity manipulation in virtual reality raises several ethical considerations that must be addressed:

Informed Consent Users should be made aware of the implications of identity manipulation in virtual environments. Informed consent is crucial, ensuring that individuals understand the potential psychological impacts and ethical dilemmas associated with adopting alternate identities.

Regulation of Virtual Spaces Developers and platform creators have a responsibility to implement measures that mitigate the risks associated with identity manipulation. This includes establishing guidelines for avatar creation and interactions, as well as mechanisms for reporting harassment and deceptive practices.

Promoting Authenticity Encouraging authentic self-expression while acknowledging the complexities of identity manipulation is essential. Virtual communities should foster environments where users feel safe to explore their identities without resorting to deception or harmful stereotypes.

Conclusion

The potential for identity manipulation in virtual reality presents a double-edged sword, offering both opportunities for self-exploration and significant ethical challenges. As users navigate the complexities of their virtual identities, it is crucial to consider the implications for authenticity, psychological well-being, and interpersonal relationships. By addressing these challenges through informed consent, regulation, and a commitment to promoting authenticity, we can harness the transformative power of virtual reality while safeguarding the integrity of individual identities.

Examining the Psychological Impact of Virtual Reality on the Self

The advent of virtual reality (VR) has opened new avenues for self-exploration and expression, but it also raises significant psychological questions about identity and self-perception. This section examines the psychological impact of VR on the self, focusing on theories of identity, potential psychological effects, and real-world implications.

Theoretical Frameworks

To understand the psychological impact of VR, we can draw upon several theories of identity formation and self-concept. One relevant framework is the **Social**

Identity Theory (Tajfel & Turner, 1979), which posits that an individual's self-concept is derived from perceived membership in social groups. In VR, users can create avatars that may or may not align with their real-world identities, leading to a complex interplay between virtual and actual selves.

Another important theory is the **Proteus Effect**, which suggests that the behavior of individuals in virtual environments can be influenced by the characteristics of their avatars (Yee & Bailenson, 2007). For instance, a user who adopts a taller avatar may exhibit more confident behavior in the virtual space, which can translate into real-world confidence.

Psychological Effects of VR on Identity

1. **Identity Exploration and Experimentation:** Virtual reality offers a unique platform for users to explore different facets of their identities. This can be particularly beneficial for individuals who may feel constrained by societal norms or expectations in the real world. For example, a user may choose an avatar that reflects a gender identity different from their biological sex, allowing for exploration of gender roles in a safe environment.

2. **Dissociation and Detachment:** While VR can facilitate identity exploration, it can also lead to dissociative experiences. Users may find themselves feeling detached from their real-world identities, particularly if they spend significant amounts of time in immersive virtual environments. This detachment can manifest in feelings of disconnection from one's body or real-life responsibilities, leading to potential psychological distress.

3. **Impact on Self-Perception:** The way individuals perceive themselves can be significantly altered by their experiences in VR. Users may develop a distorted body image based on their avatar's appearance, which can lead to body dysmorphic disorders. For instance, a user who spends time in a virtual world where beauty standards are exaggerated may begin to feel inadequate about their real-world appearance.

4. **Empathy Development:** VR has the potential to enhance empathy by allowing users to experience life from another's perspective. For example, simulations that place users in the shoes of marginalized groups can foster understanding and compassion. However, this effect is contingent upon the user's willingness to engage with the material and may not translate universally across all individuals.

Real-World Implications

The psychological impact of VR on the self has far-reaching implications. As users navigate their identities in virtual spaces, they may carry these experiences into their real lives. For instance, someone who gains confidence in VR may approach social situations differently, impacting their relationships and social interactions.

Conversely, negative experiences in VR, such as harassment or bullying, can lead to real-world consequences, including anxiety, depression, and a diminished sense of self-worth. This highlights the need for ethical considerations in VR design, ensuring that virtual environments promote healthy self-exploration and do not exacerbate psychological issues.

Conclusion

In conclusion, the psychological impact of virtual reality on the self is multifaceted and complex. While VR offers opportunities for identity exploration and empathy development, it also poses risks of dissociation and distorted self-perception. Understanding these dynamics is crucial for developing ethical guidelines that prioritize mental health and well-being in virtual environments. As VR technology continues to evolve, ongoing research is necessary to fully understand its implications for identity and the self.

Bibliography

[1] Tajfel, H., & Turner, J. C. (1979). An integrative theory of intergroup conflict. In W. G. Austin & S. Worchel (Eds.), *The social psychology of intergroup relations* (pp. 33-47). Monterey, CA: Brooks/Cole.

[2] Yee, N., & Bailenson, J. N. (2007). The Proteus Effect: The effect of transformed self-representation on behavior. *Human Communication Research*, 33(3), 271-290.

Ethical Considerations for Self-Expression in Virtual Reality

Self-expression in virtual reality (VR) serves as a powerful tool for individuals to explore and communicate their identities, beliefs, and emotions. However, the ethical implications surrounding this self-expression are complex and multifaceted. This section delves into the theoretical frameworks, challenges, and examples that illustrate the ethical considerations necessary for fostering healthy self-expression in VR environments.

Theoretical Frameworks

The discourse on self-expression in VR can be grounded in several theoretical perspectives, including symbolic interactionism, social constructivism, and postmodern identity theory.

Symbolic Interactionism posits that individuals create meaning through social interactions. In VR, users can construct and modify avatars, which serve as representations of their identities. This theory suggests that the way individuals express themselves in VR can influence their self-concept and social interactions both within and outside the virtual space.

Social Constructivism emphasizes the role of societal norms and cultural contexts in shaping self-expression. VR environments often reflect the biases and cultural narratives present in society, which can affect how individuals express themselves. For instance, an avatar designed with Eurocentric beauty standards may marginalize users from diverse backgrounds, raising questions about inclusivity and representation.

Postmodern Identity Theory challenges the notion of a singular, stable identity, advocating for a fluid understanding of self. In VR, users can experiment with various identities, allowing for exploration and expression that may not be feasible in the physical world. However, this fluidity also raises ethical concerns regarding authenticity and the potential for identity manipulation.

Challenges to Ethical Self-Expression

While VR offers unique opportunities for self-expression, several challenges must be addressed to ensure ethical practices:

1. **Privacy and Data Security** Users often share personal information to create authentic avatars, which raises concerns about data privacy. For example, platforms that collect biometric data to enhance user experience might inadvertently expose sensitive information, leading to potential misuse or exploitation.

2. **Authenticity vs. Anonymity** The ability to create anonymous avatars allows users to express themselves freely; however, it can also lead to disinhibition, resulting in harmful behaviors such as cyberbullying or harassment. The ethical dilemma lies in balancing the right to anonymity with the need for accountability.

3. **Representation and Stereotyping** The design of avatars can perpetuate stereotypes and cultural biases. For instance, if a VR platform predominantly features hypersexualized female avatars, it may reinforce harmful gender norms. Ethical self-expression requires a commitment to diverse representation that respects cultural nuances and individual identities.

4. **Psychological Impact** The immersive nature of VR can profoundly affect users' mental health. For example, individuals may develop body image issues if their avatars do not align with their real-life appearances. Ethical considerations must include the psychological effects of avatar representation and the responsibility of developers to create supportive environments.

Examples of Ethical Self-Expression in VR

Several VR platforms have taken strides toward promoting ethical self-expression:

1. **VRChat**   This social VR platform allows users to create and customize avatars, fostering a sense of community and belonging. However, it has faced challenges with harassment and hate speech. In response, VRChat implemented moderation tools and community guidelines to promote respectful interactions, emphasizing the importance of ethical behavior in self-expression.

2. **Rec Room**   Rec Room encourages creativity and self-expression through user-generated content. The platform promotes inclusivity by featuring diverse avatar options and hosting events that celebrate cultural differences. By prioritizing ethical considerations in user-generated content, Rec Room exemplifies how VR can be a space for positive self-expression.

3. **AltspaceVR**   This social VR platform focuses on creating safe spaces for marginalized communities. By hosting events that address social issues and promote dialogue, AltspaceVR demonstrates how VR can facilitate ethical self-expression while fostering understanding and empathy among users.

Conclusion

Ethical considerations for self-expression in virtual reality are essential for creating inclusive and supportive environments. By addressing challenges related to privacy, representation, and psychological impact, developers and users can work together to ensure that VR remains a space for authentic self-exploration. As the technology continues to evolve, ongoing dialogue and ethical frameworks will be crucial in navigating the complexities of self-expression in virtual reality.

Balancing Real-Life and Virtual Identities

In the age of digital interconnectedness, the distinction between real-life identities and virtual identities has become increasingly blurred. The phenomenon of balancing these identities is not merely a personal challenge; it is a cultural and ethical dilemma that warrants thorough examination. This section delves into the complexities of maintaining a coherent self-concept amidst the dual existence in physical and virtual realms.

Theoretical Framework

The concept of identity is multifaceted, encompassing various theories that help elucidate the dynamics between real-life and virtual identities. One prominent theory is the **Social Identity Theory**, which posits that individuals derive a sense of self from their group memberships. In virtual environments, users often adopt avatars that may or may not reflect their real-world identities. This adoption can lead to a fragmented self-concept, where the individual experiences dissonance between their online persona and their offline self.

Another relevant theory is **Erving Goffman's Dramaturgical Theory**, which suggests that individuals perform different roles depending on their social context. In virtual spaces, users may engage in what Goffman terms "front-stage" behavior, where they present a curated version of themselves, in contrast to the "back-stage" behavior that reflects their authentic self. This dichotomy raises questions about authenticity and the pressures of maintaining various identities.

Challenges of Identity Balancing

Balancing real-life and virtual identities presents several challenges:

- **Identity Fragmentation:** As users oscillate between their online and offline selves, they may experience a disjointed sense of identity. This fragmentation can lead to confusion and anxiety, particularly when individuals feel compelled to conform to the expectations of their virtual communities.

- **Social Comparison:** The curated nature of social media and virtual interactions can exacerbate feelings of inadequacy. Users often compare their real-life experiences to the seemingly perfect lives portrayed online, leading to decreased self-esteem and body image issues.

- **Privacy Concerns:** The need to balance identities can also raise significant privacy issues. Users may feel pressured to share personal information to maintain their virtual personas, risking their real-world privacy and security.

- **Addiction and Escapism:** The immersive nature of virtual environments can lead to escapism, where individuals prefer their online identities over their real-life counterparts. This preference can result in neglect of real-world relationships and responsibilities.

Examples of Identity Balancing

To illustrate the complexities of balancing identities, consider the case of a popular social media influencer. This individual may curate a virtual persona that embodies success, beauty, and adventure. However, the pressure to maintain this image can lead to significant stress, as the influencer grapples with the disparity between their online persona and their real-life experiences. Such cases exemplify the psychological toll that identity balancing can impose.

Another example can be drawn from online gaming communities, where players often create avatars that reflect idealized versions of themselves. While this can be empowering, it can also lead to identity conflicts when players struggle to reconcile their avatar's achievements with their real-world limitations. This phenomenon is particularly prevalent in role-playing games, where the line between character and player can become increasingly blurred.

Strategies for Balancing Identities

To navigate the complexities of balancing real-life and virtual identities, several strategies can be employed:

- **Mindfulness Practices:** Engaging in mindfulness can help individuals become more aware of their feelings and behaviors in both realms. This awareness can foster a greater sense of authenticity and self-acceptance.

- **Setting Boundaries:** Establishing clear boundaries between virtual and real-life interactions can mitigate the risks of identity fragmentation. Users should consciously decide when to engage in virtual spaces and when to disconnect.

- **Authentic Self-Presentation:** Encouraging authentic self-presentation in virtual environments can alleviate the pressures of maintaining an idealized persona. Users should feel empowered to share their true selves, including vulnerabilities and imperfections.

- **Support Networks:** Building supportive communities that prioritize mental health and well-being can provide individuals with the resources they need to navigate identity challenges. These networks can offer validation and understanding, helping users feel less isolated in their experiences.

Conclusion

Balancing real-life and virtual identities is a complex and ongoing process that requires conscious effort and reflection. As individuals navigate the digital landscape, they must be mindful of the implications of their online behaviors on their self-concept and mental health. By employing strategies that promote authenticity and well-being, users can cultivate a harmonious relationship between their real and virtual selves, ultimately leading to a more integrated and fulfilling identity experience.

$$\text{Identity Balance} = \frac{\text{Real-Life Engagement} + \text{Virtual Engagement}}{\text{Authenticity} + \text{Self-Acceptance}} \quad (7)$$

In this equation, achieving a balanced identity is contingent upon the interplay between real-life and virtual engagements, moderated by the levels of authenticity and self-acceptance experienced by the individual. Striving for equilibrium in this equation is essential for fostering a healthy relationship with both one's real and virtual identities.

Chapter Two: Morality and Virtual Reality

Ethics in Virtual Worlds

The Emergence of Virtual Ethical Systems

As virtual reality (VR) technology continues to evolve, the need for ethical frameworks within these immersive environments becomes increasingly apparent. The emergence of virtual ethical systems is not merely an academic exercise but a crucial aspect of ensuring that virtual worlds are safe, inclusive, and conducive to positive user experiences. This section will delve into the theoretical underpinnings, practical challenges, and real-world examples of virtual ethical systems.

Theoretical Foundations of Virtual Ethics

Virtual ethical systems are grounded in traditional ethical theories adapted to the unique characteristics of virtual environments. Key ethical frameworks include:

- **Utilitarianism:** This theory posits that the best action is the one that maximizes overall happiness. In virtual worlds, this could translate to designing environments that promote user well-being and minimize harm.

- **Deontological Ethics:** This approach emphasizes the importance of duty and rules. In virtual settings, it could involve establishing clear guidelines for acceptable behavior, ensuring that users understand their responsibilities.

- **Virtue Ethics:** Focusing on the character of the moral agent, this framework encourages users to develop virtuous traits such as empathy and respect within virtual interactions.

These frameworks serve as a foundation for developing ethical guidelines that govern user behavior and interactions within virtual spaces.

Challenges in Establishing Virtual Ethical Systems

While the theoretical underpinnings provide a solid base, implementing ethical systems in virtual worlds presents several challenges:

- **Anonymity and Accountability:** The anonymity afforded by virtual environments can lead to a lack of accountability. Users may engage in harmful behavior without fear of repercussions, complicating the enforcement of ethical standards.

- **Cultural Differences:** Virtual worlds often attract a global audience, leading to diverse cultural norms and values. Establishing a universally accepted ethical framework can be challenging when cultural perspectives on morality vary significantly.

- **Rapid Technological Advancement:** The fast-paced evolution of VR technology can outstrip the development of ethical guidelines, leaving gaps in regulation and oversight.

Examples of Virtual Ethical Systems in Practice

Several virtual platforms and communities have begun to implement ethical systems to address these challenges:

- **Online Gaming Communities:** Many multiplayer online games have established codes of conduct that outline acceptable behavior. For example, games like *World of Warcraft* and *Fortnite* have systems in place for reporting harassment and abusive behavior, emphasizing the importance of community standards.

- **Social Virtual Reality Platforms:** Platforms like *VRChat* have developed community-driven moderation systems. Users can report inappropriate behavior, and a community council often adjudicates disputes, promoting a self-regulating environment.

- **Educational VR Environments:** In educational settings, VR platforms are incorporating ethical discussions into their curricula. For instance, virtual simulations that explore ethical dilemmas can help users navigate complex moral landscapes, fostering critical thinking and ethical reasoning.

Future Directions for Virtual Ethical Systems

The emergence of virtual ethical systems is still in its infancy, and several future directions warrant exploration:

- **Integration of AI in Moderation:** Artificial intelligence can be leveraged to monitor user interactions and flag potential ethical violations in real-time, providing a scalable solution to maintaining ethical standards.

- **Development of Cross-Cultural Ethical Guidelines:** Collaborative efforts among international stakeholders can help create ethical frameworks that respect cultural differences while promoting universal values such as respect and empathy.

- **User Education and Engagement:** Educating users about ethical behavior in virtual environments can foster a culture of responsibility. Initiatives that promote ethical engagement, such as workshops and community discussions, can empower users to uphold ethical standards.

In conclusion, the emergence of virtual ethical systems is essential for the responsible development and use of virtual reality technologies. By grounding these systems in established ethical theories, addressing the unique challenges of virtual environments, and learning from existing examples, stakeholders can create immersive spaces that are not only entertaining but also ethical and inclusive. As we move forward, it is imperative to continue evolving these systems in response to technological advancements and cultural shifts, ensuring that virtual worlds remain safe and welcoming for all users.

Virtual Reality and Moral Responsibility

The advent of virtual reality (VR) technology has introduced a new frontier in ethical discussions surrounding moral responsibility. As users immerse themselves in virtual worlds, the question arises: who is responsible for actions taken within these digital realms? Is it the user, the developers, or the platforms that host these experiences? This section delves into the complexities of moral responsibility in virtual reality, exploring theoretical frameworks, practical implications, and real-world examples.

Theoretical Frameworks

To understand moral responsibility in virtual environments, it is essential to consider various philosophical theories. One significant framework is **consequentialism**, which posits that the morality of an action is determined by its outcomes. In the context of VR, this raises questions about the consequences of virtual actions. For instance, if a user engages in violent behavior within a VR game, does this desensitize them to violence in the real world? Research by [?] suggests a correlation between violent video games and aggressive behavior, highlighting the potential consequences of actions in virtual spaces.

Another relevant theory is **deontological ethics**, which focuses on the morality of actions themselves, regardless of their consequences. This perspective emphasizes that certain actions may be inherently wrong, even in a virtual context. For example, if a user chooses to harass another player in a VR environment, deontological ethics would argue that this action is morally unacceptable, irrespective of any potential outcomes or intentions.

Problems of Moral Responsibility in VR

The unique nature of virtual reality complicates the assignment of moral responsibility. One significant issue is the **disconnection between virtual actions and real-world consequences**. Users may feel a sense of detachment from their actions in VR, leading to a phenomenon known as the *"online disinhibition effect"* [1]. This effect can result in individuals engaging in behaviors they would typically avoid in real life, such as cyberbullying or vandalism in virtual spaces.

Moreover, the design of VR experiences can influence moral responsibility. Developers often create environments that encourage specific behaviors. For instance, a VR game that rewards players for aggressive actions may inadvertently promote a culture of violence. This raises ethical questions about the responsibility of developers in shaping user behavior. Should they be held accountable for the moral implications of their designs? As [?] posits, developers have a duty to consider the ethical ramifications of their virtual worlds.

Real-World Examples

Several notable incidents illustrate the complexities of moral responsibility in virtual reality. One such example is the case of **"VR Chat"**, a social VR platform where users can create and interact in various environments. Instances of harassment and abuse have been reported, prompting discussions about user accountability and platform responsibility. In response, VR Chat implemented community guidelines to address toxic behavior, emphasizing the role of both users and developers in fostering a safe environment.

Another example is the controversy surrounding the game **"Beat Saber"**, where players use virtual lightsabers to slice through blocks. While the game is widely regarded as a fun and engaging experience, concerns have been raised about its potential to normalize violence. Critics argue that even seemingly innocuous games can contribute to desensitization, blurring the lines between acceptable virtual behavior and real-world morality.

Conclusion

In conclusion, the question of moral responsibility in virtual reality is multifaceted, involving various theoretical frameworks and real-world implications. As users navigate these immersive environments, the potential for disconnection from reality complicates the assignment of responsibility. Developers and platforms also bear a significant ethical burden in shaping user experiences. As VR technology continues to evolve, ongoing discussions about moral responsibility will be essential in fostering a safe and ethical virtual landscape.

The Role of Virtual Law in Governing Virtual Worlds

The advent of virtual reality (VR) has not only transformed how we interact with technology but has also raised complex legal and ethical questions regarding governance within these immersive environments. As individuals engage in virtual worlds, the need for a structured legal framework becomes imperative to address the unique challenges posed by these digital realms. This section explores the role of virtual law in governing virtual worlds, examining its theoretical foundations, practical challenges, and illustrative examples.

Theoretical Foundations of Virtual Law

Virtual law can be understood through various theoretical lenses, including legal positivism, natural law, and social contract theory. Legal positivism posits that laws are rules created by human beings and are not necessarily tied to moral considerations. In virtual worlds, this perspective supports the notion that virtual laws can be established by the developers or governing bodies of these environments, irrespective of moral implications.

Conversely, natural law theory argues that laws should reflect moral principles inherent in human nature. This perspective raises questions about the ethical implications of virtual laws, particularly in relation to issues such as harassment, discrimination, and user privacy. Social contract theory, on the other hand, suggests that individuals consent to certain rules and regulations in exchange for protection and benefits within the virtual space. This concept is particularly relevant in understanding user agreements and community guidelines that govern behavior in virtual worlds.

Key Challenges in Virtual Law

Despite the theoretical underpinnings, several challenges arise in the application of virtual law:

- **Jurisdictional Issues:** Virtual worlds often transcend geographical boundaries, complicating the enforcement of laws. Users from different countries may engage in activities that are legal in one jurisdiction but illegal in another. For example, virtual property theft may be treated differently under various national laws, leading to ambiguity in legal recourse.

- **Enforcement Mechanisms:** The enforcement of virtual laws presents unique difficulties. Unlike traditional legal systems, virtual environments may lack robust mechanisms for monitoring and enforcing compliance. This can lead to a culture of impunity where users feel free to engage in harmful behavior without fear of repercussions.

- **User Anonymity:** Many virtual worlds allow for user anonymity, complicating accountability. While anonymity can enhance freedom of expression, it can also facilitate harassment and illegal activities. Balancing user privacy with the need for accountability remains a significant challenge.

- **Evolving Technologies:** The rapid pace of technological advancement in VR often outstrips existing legal frameworks. Laws that govern virtual interactions may quickly become outdated, necessitating continuous adaptation and revision.

Examples of Virtual Law in Action

Several virtual worlds have begun to implement their own legal systems to address these challenges:

1. **Second Life:** This virtual environment has developed a comprehensive legal framework that includes user agreements, community standards, and a dispute

resolution system. Users can engage in virtual property transactions, and the platform has established rules regarding intellectual property rights, ensuring that creators retain ownership of their digital assets.

2. **Fortnite:** In the gaming world, Fortnite has introduced a code of conduct that governs player behavior. Violations can result in penalties ranging from temporary suspensions to permanent bans, demonstrating an effort to maintain a safe and respectful environment for all players.

3. **Decentraland:** As a blockchain-based virtual world, Decentraland operates under a decentralized governance model. Users can participate in decision-making processes regarding land use, community standards, and resource allocation, illustrating a novel approach to virtual law that emphasizes user agency and collective governance.

Future Directions for Virtual Law

The evolution of virtual law must consider the following future directions:

- **International Collaboration:** To address jurisdictional challenges, international cooperation among governments, legal experts, and technology developers is essential. Establishing a framework for cross-border legal agreements can facilitate the enforcement of laws in virtual spaces.

- **Technological Solutions:** Leveraging technology, such as blockchain and smart contracts, can enhance transparency and accountability in virtual law. These tools can provide immutable records of transactions and interactions, aiding in dispute resolution and legal enforcement.

- **User Education:** Educating users about their rights and responsibilities within virtual worlds is crucial. Promoting awareness of virtual laws and community standards can foster a culture of respect and accountability among users.

- **Adaptive Legal Frameworks:** Legal systems governing virtual worlds must be flexible and adaptable to keep pace with technological advancements. Policymakers should engage with technologists and users to develop laws that reflect the dynamic nature of virtual environments.

In conclusion, the role of virtual law in governing virtual worlds is multifaceted and complex. As these digital realms continue to evolve, so too must the legal frameworks that support them. By addressing theoretical foundations, overcoming challenges, and learning from existing examples, we can pave the way for a more equitable and just virtual landscape that respects the rights and responsibilities of all users.

Cultivating Empathy and Compassion in Virtual Reality

Empathy and compassion are essential components of human interaction and understanding. In the context of Virtual Reality (VR), these qualities can be both fostered and challenged. This section will explore how VR can be a powerful tool for cultivating empathy and compassion, while also addressing the potential pitfalls and ethical considerations involved.

Theoretical Framework

Empathy is defined as the ability to understand and share the feelings of another. It can be divided into two main components: cognitive empathy, which is the ability to understand another's perspective, and emotional empathy, which is the capacity to physically feel what another person is feeling. [?] In VR, the immersive nature of the medium allows users to experience situations from different perspectives, potentially enhancing both cognitive and emotional empathy.

One relevant theory is the **Theory of Mind**, which posits that individuals can attribute mental states to themselves and others. VR can simulate experiences that challenge users' existing beliefs and assumptions, thereby expanding their understanding of others' experiences. For example, users may assume the avatar of a person from a marginalized community, allowing them to experience life through that individual's lens, which can significantly enhance empathetic understanding.

Empathy Induction through Immersion

Research has shown that immersive experiences can lead to increased empathy. For instance, a study by [?] demonstrated that participants who experienced a VR simulation of a homeless person's life reported a greater understanding of homelessness and a desire to help those in need. This phenomenon can be attributed to the **embodiment effect**, where users feel as though they are physically present in the virtual environment, leading to a more profound emotional connection to the experiences portrayed.

Examples of VR Empathy Applications

Several VR applications have been developed specifically to cultivate empathy:

- **The Wave VR:** This platform allows users to experience life as a refugee, navigating challenges and hardships faced by displaced individuals. Users reported increased awareness and empathy towards refugees after participating in the experience.

- **The Empathy Lab:** This initiative uses VR to simulate the experiences of individuals with disabilities, enabling users to understand the barriers faced by these individuals in everyday life. Participants have shown increased compassion and a desire to advocate for accessibility improvements in their communities.

- **VR for Good:** This program focuses on social issues, creating immersive experiences that highlight various humanitarian crises. By placing users in the shoes of those affected, the program aims to inspire action and support for relevant causes.

Challenges and Ethical Considerations

While VR has the potential to cultivate empathy, there are challenges and ethical considerations that must be addressed:

- **Emotional Overload:** Prolonged exposure to distressing scenarios in VR can lead to emotional fatigue or desensitization. It is essential to balance immersive experiences with appropriate debriefing and support.

- **Misrepresentation:** If VR experiences are not accurately representing the lives of others, they can perpetuate stereotypes or reinforce biases rather than challenge them. Developers must ensure that their content is created in collaboration with the communities being represented.

- **Commercialization of Empathy:** There is a risk that VR experiences designed to cultivate empathy could be commodified, reducing genuine emotional engagement to a mere product. This raises questions about the authenticity of the empathy generated through such experiences.

- **Consent and Agency:** Users should have the right to choose their experiences and should be informed of the emotional content they may encounter. It is crucial to ensure that users can opt-out or have control over their virtual interactions.

Future Directions

Moving forward, developers and researchers must prioritize ethical considerations when creating VR experiences aimed at fostering empathy and compassion. This includes:

- Engaging with communities to ensure accurate representation and authentic narratives.

- Implementing feedback mechanisms that allow users to express their emotional responses and suggest improvements to the VR experiences.

- Conducting longitudinal studies to assess the long-term impact of VR empathy experiences on real-life behavior and attitudes.

In conclusion, while Virtual Reality holds significant promise for cultivating empathy and compassion, it is imperative to approach its development and implementation thoughtfully. By addressing the challenges and ethical considerations outlined in this section, VR can become a transformative tool for enhancing understanding and fostering connections among individuals from diverse backgrounds.

Tackling Issues of Harm and Violence in Virtual Environments

The advent of virtual reality (VR) has opened up new frontiers for immersive experiences, but it has also raised significant ethical concerns, particularly regarding harm and violence within these environments. This section aims to explore the various dimensions of harm and violence in virtual worlds, the theoretical frameworks that underpin these issues, and the strategies that can be employed to mitigate such risks.

Theoretical Frameworks

The discussion of harm and violence in virtual environments can be framed through several theoretical lenses, including social learning theory, desensitization theory, and the theory of moral disengagement.

Social Learning Theory posits that individuals learn behaviors through observation and imitation of others, particularly in environments that reward such behaviors. In VR, users can witness and replicate violent actions without immediate consequences, leading to the normalization of aggression. Bandura's

(1977) work on observational learning suggests that repeated exposure to violence in VR can lead to increased aggression in real life, as users may begin to view such behavior as acceptable.

Desensitization Theory suggests that repeated exposure to violence can lead to a diminished emotional response. In the context of VR, users who frequently engage in violent scenarios may become desensitized to real-world violence. This phenomenon raises concerns about the potential for VR to erode empathy and compassion, which are crucial for moral reasoning and ethical behavior.

Moral Disengagement refers to the cognitive processes that allow individuals to engage in harmful behaviors without feeling moral responsibility. In virtual environments, users may rationalize violent actions as "just part of the game" or "not real," which can lead to a slippery slope of ethical violations. Bandura's (1990) model of moral disengagement highlights mechanisms such as dehumanization and diffusion of responsibility, which can be exacerbated in immersive VR settings.

Problems Associated with Harm and Violence

The potential for harm and violence in VR is not merely theoretical; it manifests in various problematic ways:

- **Harassment and Bullying:** Just as in real life, virtual environments can become breeding grounds for harassment. Users may experience bullying through verbal abuse or aggressive behavior from others, which can lead to psychological harm and a toxic community atmosphere.

- **Desensitization to Violence:** Users who frequently engage in violent VR experiences may become desensitized, leading to diminished empathy towards real-world violence. This desensitization can create a disconnect between virtual actions and their real-world implications.

- **Escalation of Violence:** The immersive nature of VR can lead to an escalation of violent behavior. Users may feel emboldened to act out in ways they would not in real life, leading to increasingly aggressive actions within the virtual space.

- **Psychological Impact:** Exposure to violent content in VR can have lasting psychological effects, including anxiety, depression, and post-traumatic stress disorder (PTSD). The immersive experience can make violent scenarios feel more real, intensifying their emotional impact.

Examples of Harm and Violence in VR

Several instances highlight the issues of harm and violence in virtual environments:

- **VR Games:** Many popular VR games, such as "Beat Saber" and "Pavlov VR," include violent content. While these games are often framed as entertainment, the repeated exposure to violence can lead to the normalization of aggressive behaviors among players.

- **Sexual Harassment:** Reports of sexual harassment in VR platforms, such as VRChat, have raised alarms about user safety. Instances of unwanted virtual touching or verbal harassment can lead to significant psychological distress for victims.

- **Real-World Consequences:** In extreme cases, individuals have attempted to replicate violent acts from VR in real life, leading to tragic outcomes. This phenomenon underscores the potential for VR to influence real-world behavior in dangerous ways.

Strategies for Mitigating Harm and Violence

To address the issues of harm and violence in virtual environments, several strategies can be employed:

- **Community Guidelines and Reporting Mechanisms:** Establishing clear community guidelines that prohibit harassment and violent behavior is essential. Implementing robust reporting mechanisms allows users to report abusive behavior and helps maintain a safe environment.

- **Empathy Training:** Developers can incorporate empathy-building exercises within VR experiences. By allowing users to experience scenarios from different perspectives, they may develop a greater understanding of the impact of violence on others.

- **Content Rating Systems:** Similar to film and video game ratings, a content rating system for VR experiences can help users make informed choices about the types of content they engage with. This transparency can empower users to avoid violent content that may be harmful to their well-being.

- **User Education:** Educating users about the potential psychological impacts of engaging with violent content can raise awareness and promote responsible consumption of VR experiences. This education can include information on the effects of desensitization and the importance of empathy.

Conclusion

The issues of harm and violence in virtual environments present complex ethical challenges that require careful consideration. By understanding the theoretical frameworks that underpin these issues, recognizing the problems associated with violence, and implementing effective strategies for mitigation, we can foster safer and more responsible virtual worlds. The goal is not to eliminate all instances of violence in VR but to create an environment where users can engage with content in a way that is mindful of its potential impacts, both in the virtual realm and beyond.

Virtual Reality and the Question of Morally Grey Choices

Virtual Reality (VR) has emerged as a powerful medium that allows users to immerse themselves in experiences that can challenge their ethical frameworks. Within these virtual environments, users often encounter scenarios that present morally grey choices—situations where the distinction between right and wrong is blurred. This section explores the implications of these morally ambiguous situations in virtual reality, drawing on ethical theories, real-world examples, and the psychological effects they can have on users.

Understanding Morally Grey Choices

Morally grey choices are decisions that do not have a clear ethical direction; they can be seen as justifiable from one perspective while being condemnable from another. Such choices often arise in complex social situations where values conflict. In VR, these scenarios can be designed to elicit emotional responses, forcing players to confront their moral beliefs in ways that might not occur in real life.

Ethical Theories and Frameworks

To understand the implications of morally grey choices in VR, we can apply several ethical theories:

- **Utilitarianism:** This theory posits that the best action is the one that maximizes overall happiness. In a VR scenario, a player may face a choice between sacrificing one character to save many others. Here, the utilitarian calculation would weigh the happiness of the majority against the suffering of the individual.

- **Deontological Ethics:** This perspective emphasizes the importance of following moral rules or duties regardless of the consequences. A player might grapple with a scenario where lying could save lives, which would conflict with a deontological stance that prioritizes truth-telling.

- **Virtue Ethics:** This approach focuses on the character of the moral agent rather than on rules or consequences. In VR, a player might reflect on how their choices align with their values and the kind of person they aspire to be.

The interplay of these theories can create a rich tapestry of moral dilemmas in VR, prompting players to navigate their ethical beliefs actively.

Examples of Morally Grey Choices in VR

Several VR games and experiences exemplify morally grey choices:

- **The Walking Dead: VR Edition:** In this game, players frequently face decisions that pit survival against morality. For instance, players may choose to help a stranger at the risk of their own group's safety. The choice can lead to varied outcomes, forcing players to weigh the value of human life against their own survival.

- **Detroit: Become Human:** This narrative-driven game presents players with choices that challenge their understanding of freedom and autonomy. Players must decide whether to prioritize the welfare of androids seeking freedom or the societal norms that oppress them. Each choice has significant consequences, not just for the characters but also for the player's moral standing.

- **Papers, Please:** In this game, players assume the role of an immigration officer tasked with processing individuals seeking entry into a dystopian country. Players face morally ambiguous decisions about whether to allow entry to individuals who may pose a threat or deny entry to innocent people, forcing them to confront their own biases and values.

Psychological Implications

The immersion of VR can amplify the psychological impact of morally grey choices. Research has shown that engaging with morally complex scenarios can lead to:

- **Increased Empathy:** Players may develop a deeper understanding of the perspectives of others, leading to increased empathy. This can be particularly beneficial in scenarios that require players to consider the consequences of their actions on others.

- **Cognitive Dissonance:** Players may experience discomfort when their actions in VR conflict with their real-world moral beliefs. This dissonance can lead to reflection and, potentially, a reassessment of their values.

- **Desensitization:** Conversely, repeated exposure to morally grey choices can lead to desensitization, where players become numb to the ethical implications of their decisions. This raises concerns about the long-term effects of engaging with such content.

Ethical Considerations for Developers

Given the potential impact of morally grey choices in VR, developers must consider several ethical implications:

- **Designing with Intent:** Developers should be mindful of the scenarios they create and the messages they convey. It is crucial to avoid trivializing serious moral dilemmas and to promote thoughtful engagement with ethical issues.

- **Informed Consent:** Players should be made aware of the nature of the moral dilemmas they will face. Providing content warnings or briefings can help prepare players for the emotional weight of their choices.

- **Encouraging Reflection:** Incorporating mechanisms that encourage players to reflect on their choices can foster deeper engagement with the ethical dimensions of the game. This can include post-game discussions or reflective prompts that challenge players to think critically about their decisions.

Conclusion

The question of morally grey choices in virtual reality presents both opportunities and challenges. As VR technology continues to evolve, the potential for immersive experiences that engage players in complex ethical dilemmas will grow. Understanding the implications of these choices is essential for both players and developers. By fostering a space for ethical reflection and promoting responsible design, the VR community can navigate the complexities of morality in virtual worlds, ultimately enriching the player's experience and understanding of their own values.

The Influence of Virtual Experiences on Real-Life Morality

The advent of virtual reality (VR) has revolutionized how individuals engage with moral dilemmas, presenting unique opportunities and challenges for understanding morality in a digital context. This section explores the intricate relationship between virtual experiences and real-life moral behavior, drawing from various theoretical frameworks, empirical research, and practical examples.

Theoretical Frameworks

To understand the influence of virtual experiences on real-life morality, it is essential to consider several theoretical frameworks, including Social Learning Theory, the Theory of Planned Behavior, and the concept of Moral Disengagement.

Social Learning Theory posits that individuals learn behaviors through observation and imitation of others, particularly in social contexts. In VR environments, users often observe avatars and characters engaging in moral or immoral actions. For instance, a player who witnesses a character committing a virtual crime without repercussions may internalize this behavior, affecting their moral compass in real life. Bandura (1977) emphasized that individuals are more likely to imitate behaviors they see rewarded, which can lead to desensitization towards violence or unethical actions.

Theory of Planned Behavior suggests that an individual's intention to perform a behavior is influenced by their attitudes, subjective norms, and perceived behavioral control. In virtual environments, users may encounter scenarios that challenge their moral beliefs. For example, a VR simulation that places users in a position where they must choose between saving a character or saving resources can shape their attitudes towards altruism and self-interest. If users consistently engage in self-serving choices in VR, it may lead to a shift in their real-life moral intentions.

Moral Disengagement refers to the cognitive processes that allow individuals to detach from their moral standards. Bandura (1991) identified several mechanisms of moral disengagement, including moral justification, displacement of responsibility, and dehumanization. VR can facilitate moral disengagement by immersing users in environments where they can act without facing real-world consequences. For example, a user who participates in a violent game may rationalize their actions as mere entertainment, potentially leading to a diminished sense of responsibility for violent behavior in real life.

Empirical Research

Numerous studies have explored the connection between virtual experiences and real-life morality. Research by Ratan and Ritterfeld (2009) demonstrated that immersive virtual experiences could significantly influence users' attitudes towards real-world issues. In their study, participants who engaged in a VR simulation that highlighted the struggles of marginalized communities reported increased empathy and a greater willingness to support social justice initiatives.

Conversely, other studies have indicated that exposure to violent virtual experiences can lead to desensitization and an increase in aggressive behavior. Anderson et al. (2010) conducted a meta-analysis revealing that individuals who frequently played violent video games exhibited higher levels of aggression and lower levels of empathy in real-life situations. This finding raises concerns about the potential for VR to reinforce negative moral behaviors.

Practical Examples

Practical examples further illustrate the influence of virtual experiences on real-life morality. Consider the case of *The Walking Dead: Saints & Sinners*, a VR game that places players in morally ambiguous situations where they must make difficult choices about survival. Players often face dilemmas that challenge their ethical beliefs, such as deciding whether to help a stranger or secure resources for themselves. The decisions made in the game can reflect and potentially alter players' moral frameworks, leading to discussions about the implications of such experiences.

In contrast, VR applications designed for empathy training, such as *The Empathy Experiment*, allow users to experience life from the perspective of marginalized individuals. Research indicates that participants who engaged with these simulations reported increased empathy and a stronger commitment to social justice issues. These contrasting examples highlight the dual potential of VR to either reinforce negative behaviors or promote positive moral development.

Challenges and Considerations

While the influence of virtual experiences on real-life morality presents exciting opportunities, it also poses several challenges. One significant concern is the potential for VR to blur the lines between fantasy and reality. Users may struggle to reconcile their virtual actions with their moral beliefs, leading to confusion about acceptable behavior in real life. Additionally, the immersive nature of VR can create a sense of detachment, reducing the emotional impact of moral decisions.

Another challenge lies in the ethical design of virtual experiences. Developers must consider the moral implications of the scenarios they create and strive to promote ethical behavior rather than exploitative or harmful actions. This responsibility extends to educators and policymakers, who must navigate the complexities of integrating VR into curricula and public policy.

Conclusion

In conclusion, the influence of virtual experiences on real-life morality is a multifaceted issue that warrants careful examination. Theoretical frameworks such as Social Learning Theory, the Theory of Planned Behavior, and Moral Disengagement provide valuable insights into how virtual environments can shape moral behavior. Empirical research and practical examples further illustrate the dual potential of VR to either reinforce negative behaviors or promote positive moral development. As VR continues to evolve, it is imperative to consider the ethical implications of these experiences and their impact on individuals' moral frameworks in the real world.

The Limits of Morality in Virtual Reality

The advent of virtual reality (VR) has transformed the landscape of interpersonal interactions, allowing users to engage in immersive experiences that challenge traditional ethical frameworks. While VR has the potential to cultivate empathy and foster moral growth, it also presents unique challenges that complicate our understanding of morality. This section explores the limits of morality in virtual reality, examining the theoretical underpinnings, practical problems, and illustrative examples that highlight these constraints.

Theoretical Frameworks of Morality

To understand the limits of morality in VR, it is essential to consider various ethical theories that inform our moral judgments. Two prominent theories are utilitarianism and deontological ethics.

- **Utilitarianism** posits that the morality of an action is determined by its consequences, specifically the overall happiness it produces. In VR, this raises questions about whether actions that may cause harm in the virtual world can be justified if they lead to greater enjoyment for the majority of users.

ETHICS IN VIRTUAL WORLDS

- **Deontological ethics**, on the other hand, asserts that certain actions are inherently right or wrong, regardless of their outcomes. This perspective challenges users in VR to consider the moral implications of their actions, even when they are shielded from real-world consequences.

The interplay between these ethical frameworks reveals a fundamental tension in VR: actions that may be deemed acceptable in a virtual context could be considered immoral in reality. This dichotomy raises critical questions about the nature of moral responsibility in virtual environments.

Practical Problems in Virtual Morality

One of the primary challenges of morality in VR is the phenomenon of *disassociation*. Users often perceive their virtual actions as separate from their real-world selves, leading to a detachment from moral accountability. This disassociation can result in behaviors that individuals would typically deem unacceptable in real life, such as virtual violence or harassment.

$$\text{Disassociation} = \frac{\text{Virtual Actions}}{\text{Real-World Accountability}} \qquad (8)$$

As the equation suggests, as virtual actions increase, the sense of accountability may diminish, leading to moral disengagement. This moral disengagement can be exacerbated by the anonymity that VR often provides, allowing users to act without fear of social repercussions.

Another significant issue is the *moral grey area* that virtual experiences can create. Users may encounter scenarios where the ethical implications are ambiguous, forcing them to navigate complex moral dilemmas. For instance, a player might be faced with a choice to betray a virtual ally for personal gain, raising questions about loyalty and ethics in a space where the stakes seem low.

Examples of Moral Limits in VR

Several case studies illustrate the limits of morality in VR. One notable example is the game *Grand Theft Auto V*, which allows players to engage in criminal activities without real-world consequences. While some players argue that the game serves as a form of escapism, others contend that it desensitizes individuals to violence and ethical violations.

Similarly, the VR experience *VR Chat* has garnered attention for instances of harassment and bullying, where users exploit the immersive environment to engage in harmful behaviors. These examples underscore the potential for VR to blur the lines between acceptable and unacceptable conduct, challenging our moral frameworks.

The Role of Virtual Law

As the limits of morality in VR become increasingly apparent, there is a growing discourse on the establishment of virtual laws to govern behavior within these spaces. However, the implementation of such laws raises further questions about jurisdiction, enforcement, and the effectiveness of legal frameworks in addressing moral transgressions.

$$\text{Effectiveness of Virtual Law} = \frac{\text{User Compliance}}{\text{Enforcement Mechanisms}} \quad (9)$$

This equation indicates that the effectiveness of virtual law is contingent upon user compliance and the presence of robust enforcement mechanisms. Without a clear framework for accountability, the moral limits of VR may continue to expand, leading to a culture of impunity.

Conclusion

In conclusion, the limits of morality in virtual reality present significant challenges that require careful consideration. The disassociation from real-world consequences, the existence of moral grey areas, and the need for effective virtual laws all contribute to a complex ethical landscape. As VR technology continues to evolve, it is imperative for developers, users, and ethicists to engage in ongoing dialogue to address these limitations and promote a more responsible virtual culture. By fostering an understanding of the ethical implications of our actions in virtual spaces, we can work towards a future where morality transcends the boundaries of reality and virtuality.

Reflecting on the Ethical Implications of Immersive Storytelling

Immersive storytelling in virtual reality (VR) presents unique ethical challenges and implications that merit careful consideration. As users engage with narratives in an immersive environment, the boundaries between fiction and reality blur, raising questions about the responsibilities of creators, the impact on participants, and the potential for manipulation.

The Nature of Immersive Storytelling

Immersive storytelling leverages the capabilities of VR to create experiences that are not only visually engaging but also emotionally resonant. According to Murray (1997), immersive narratives allow users to become active participants rather than passive observers, leading to a deeper emotional connection with the story. This heightened engagement can lead to transformative experiences, as users may find themselves empathizing with characters or situations that reflect real-world issues.

Ethical Considerations in Narrative Design

The design of immersive narratives must consider several ethical dimensions:

- **Representation and Stereotyping:** Immersive storytelling often involves the portrayal of diverse characters and cultures. Ethical storytelling necessitates authentic representation to avoid perpetuating stereotypes. For instance, the game *Far Cry 3* faced criticism for its portrayal of indigenous cultures, leading to discussions about cultural sensitivity in narrative design.

- **User Agency and Consent:** In immersive environments, users may encounter scenarios that challenge their moral beliefs or force them to make difficult decisions. The ethical implications of user agency must be addressed, ensuring that users are aware of the potential emotional impacts of their choices. Games like *Detroit: Become Human* exemplify this issue, as players navigate morally ambiguous situations that can elicit strong emotional responses.

- **Psychological Impact:** The immersive nature of VR can lead to significant psychological effects, including trauma or distress. Developers must consider the potential for harm when creating narratives that involve sensitive topics such as violence, loss, or discrimination. The game *Hellblade: Senua's Sacrifice* addresses mental health issues through its narrative, but it also raises questions about the ethics of depicting such experiences in a way that could be triggering for some players.

The Role of Empathy in Immersive Storytelling

One of the most compelling aspects of immersive storytelling is its potential to foster empathy. Studies have shown that experiencing narratives in VR can enhance emotional engagement and understanding of different perspectives (Harris et al., 2018). However, this raises ethical questions about the manipulation of emotions. For instance, while a narrative might aim to generate empathy towards a marginalized group, it could also risk exploiting their suffering for entertainment purposes.

The Dangers of Manipulation

The potential for manipulation in immersive storytelling is significant. As users become more immersed, the risk of emotional and psychological manipulation increases. This raises ethical concerns regarding the intentions of creators. For example, a narrative designed to elicit fear or anxiety could lead to lasting psychological effects. Developers must tread carefully, balancing the desire to evoke strong emotions with the responsibility to protect users from potential harm.

Case Studies in Immersive Storytelling

Several case studies illustrate the ethical implications of immersive storytelling:

- **The Walking Dead: Saints & Sinners** presents players with morally complex choices that impact the game's outcome. While it offers a rich narrative experience, it also challenges players to confront the consequences of their actions, prompting discussions about morality in virtual environments.

- **The Night Cafe** immerses users in a surreal experience inspired by Vincent van Gogh's artwork. The ethical implications here lie in the representation of an artist's mental state and the potential for romanticizing mental illness without proper context or sensitivity.

Conclusion

In conclusion, the ethical implications of immersive storytelling in virtual reality are multifaceted and complex. As creators continue to explore the potential of VR narratives, it is crucial to prioritize ethical considerations in design, representation, and user experience. By fostering a deeper understanding of the responsibilities inherent in immersive storytelling, developers can create experiences that not only engage users but also contribute positively to societal discourse.

$$\text{Empathy}_{VR} = f(\text{Immersion, Narrative Complexity, User Agency}) \quad (10)$$

This equation illustrates the relationship between empathy in virtual reality and factors such as immersion, narrative complexity, and user agency. As the field of immersive storytelling evolves, ongoing reflection on these ethical implications will be essential to ensure that the medium is used responsibly and thoughtfully.

Promoting Ethical Behavior in Virtual Communities

In the rapidly evolving landscape of virtual reality (VR), fostering ethical behavior within virtual communities has emerged as a critical challenge. As users immerse themselves in these digital environments, the potential for both positive and negative interactions increases, necessitating a robust framework for promoting ethics. This section explores the theoretical foundations, challenges, and practical strategies for encouraging ethical conduct in virtual spaces.

Theoretical Foundations of Ethical Behavior

The promotion of ethical behavior in virtual communities can be anchored in several ethical theories, including:

- **Utilitarianism:** This theory posits that the best action is one that maximizes overall happiness or utility. In virtual communities, this translates to creating environments that prioritize user well-being and minimize harm. For example, implementing moderation policies that reduce toxic behavior can enhance the overall experience for all users.

- **Deontological Ethics:** This approach emphasizes adherence to rules and duties. In virtual settings, establishing clear codes of conduct can guide users in their interactions. For instance, many online games have strict rules against cheating and harassment, reinforcing a sense of responsibility among players.

- **Virtue Ethics:** Focusing on the character of individuals rather than specific actions, virtue ethics encourages users to cultivate traits such as empathy, respect, and integrity. Initiatives that reward positive behavior—such as recognizing users who contribute constructively—can promote a virtuous culture.

Challenges to Ethical Behavior in Virtual Communities

Despite the theoretical frameworks available, several challenges hinder the promotion of ethical behavior in virtual communities:

- **Anonymity and Disinhibition:** The anonymity afforded by virtual environments can lead to disinhibition, where individuals engage in behavior they would avoid in real life. Research indicates that anonymity can exacerbate aggression and reduce accountability [1]. For example, online trolls often exploit this anonymity to harass others without facing real-world consequences.

- **Lack of Regulation:** Many virtual communities operate without stringent regulations, leading to a culture where unethical behavior can flourish. The absence of oversight can result in environments where harassment, discrimination, and exploitation are common. For instance, platforms like Second Life have faced criticism for inadequate measures to protect users from harassment.

- **Cultural Differences:** Virtual communities often comprise users from diverse cultural backgrounds, each with varying norms and values. This diversity can lead to misunderstandings and conflicts regarding acceptable behavior. For example, what is considered humorous in one culture may be perceived as offensive in another, complicating efforts to establish universal ethical standards.

Strategies for Promoting Ethical Behavior

To address these challenges, several strategies can be employed to foster ethical behavior in virtual communities:

- **Establishing Clear Guidelines:** Creating and disseminating clear codes of conduct is essential for guiding user behavior. These guidelines should outline acceptable and unacceptable actions, providing users with a framework for engagement. Platforms like Discord have successfully implemented community guidelines that emphasize respect and inclusivity.

- **Implementing Moderation Tools:** Effective moderation is crucial for maintaining ethical standards. This can include automated systems to detect and address harmful behavior, as well as human moderators who can intervene in real-time. For example, Twitch employs both automated filters and human moderators to manage chat interactions, reducing instances of toxic behavior.

- **Encouraging Positive Reinforcement:** Recognizing and rewarding ethical behavior can cultivate a culture of respect and empathy. This can be achieved through systems that highlight users who contribute positively to the community, such as through commendations or leaderboards. For instance, platforms like Reddit use upvote systems to promote constructive contributions.

- **Fostering Education and Awareness:** Providing users with resources and training on ethical behavior can enhance their understanding of the impact of their actions. Workshops, webinars, and informational campaigns can educate users about the importance of empathy and respect in virtual interactions. Initiatives like "Digital Citizenship" programs in educational settings exemplify this approach.

- **Promoting Inclusive Design:** Developing virtual environments that are inclusive and accessible can mitigate issues related to discrimination and exclusion. This includes ensuring that platforms are designed with diverse user needs in mind, thereby fostering a sense of belonging. For instance, VR platforms that incorporate features for users with disabilities demonstrate a commitment to inclusivity.

Conclusion

Promoting ethical behavior in virtual communities is essential for creating safe and inclusive environments for all users. By leveraging theoretical frameworks, addressing challenges, and implementing effective strategies, developers and community leaders can foster a culture of respect and empathy. As virtual reality continues to evolve, prioritizing ethics will be crucial in shaping the future of these digital spaces.

Bibliography

[Suler(2004)] Suler, J. (2004). The online disinhibition effect. *CyberPsychology & Behavior*, 7(3), 321-326.

Chapter Three: Cultural Perspectives on Virtual Reality

Cultural Diversity in Virtual Worlds

Cultural Representation in Virtual Environments

Cultural representation in virtual environments is a critical aspect of how individuals and communities engage with and experience virtual reality (VR). As virtual worlds become increasingly immersive and influential, the way cultures are depicted, interpreted, and interacted with in these spaces raises important questions about authenticity, ownership, and the potential for cultural appropriation. This section explores the theoretical frameworks surrounding cultural representation, the challenges faced by diverse communities, and the implications for ethical practices in the development of virtual environments.

Theoretical Frameworks

The study of cultural representation in virtual environments can be grounded in several theoretical perspectives, including postcolonial theory, cultural studies, and critical race theory. These frameworks help to unpack the complexities of how cultures are portrayed and the power dynamics at play in virtual spaces.

Postcolonial theory, for instance, examines the lingering effects of colonialism on cultural identities and representations. In the context of VR, this theory raises questions about who controls the narratives and images of marginalized cultures. Edward Said's concept of *Orientalism* (1978) illustrates how Western representations of Eastern cultures often perpetuate stereotypes and inaccuracies, leading to a distorted understanding of those cultures. In virtual environments, similar dynamics can emerge, where developers from dominant cultures create representations of minority cultures without adequate understanding or respect for their complexities.

Cultural studies provide another lens through which to analyze representation in VR. This field emphasizes the role of media in shaping cultural identities and the importance of audience interpretation. Stuart Hall's encoding/decoding model posits that media messages are encoded by creators with certain meanings but are decoded by audiences in diverse ways, influenced by their cultural backgrounds and experiences. In virtual environments, the encoding of cultural symbols and narratives can lead to varied interpretations, which may reinforce or challenge existing stereotypes.

Critical race theory also plays a significant role in understanding cultural representation in VR. This perspective highlights how race and ethnicity intersect with other social categories, such as class and gender, to shape experiences in virtual spaces. By examining the representation of racial and ethnic minorities in VR, researchers can uncover systemic biases and advocate for more equitable portrayals.

Challenges of Cultural Representation

Despite the potential for VR to serve as a platform for cultural expression and exchange, significant challenges remain. One of the primary issues is the risk of cultural appropriation, where elements of a marginalized culture are adopted by individuals from a dominant culture without understanding or respecting their significance. This can lead to commodification and trivialization of cultural practices, as seen in the use of Indigenous symbols and attire in gaming without proper context or acknowledgment of their meanings.

Moreover, the lack of diversity among VR developers and creators can exacerbate these issues. When predominantly homogenous teams design virtual environments, they may inadvertently reinforce stereotypes or exclude certain cultural narratives altogether. This can result in virtual spaces that do not accurately reflect the richness and diversity of human experiences, leading to a sense of alienation for users from underrepresented backgrounds.

Another challenge is the representation of cultural practices that may not translate well into virtual formats. For example, traditional ceremonies or rituals may be difficult to accurately depict in VR due to their intricate cultural significance and the need for contextual understanding. This raises ethical questions about whether and how to represent such practices in virtual environments.

Examples of Cultural Representation in VR

Several examples illustrate both the potential and pitfalls of cultural representation in virtual environments. One notable case is the VR experience *The Night Cafe*, which recreates the iconic painting by Vincent van Gogh. This immersive experience allows users to explore a virtual representation of the artwork, but it also raises questions about the authenticity of the representation and the cultural context of the artist's work. While it provides an opportunity for engagement with art, it may also risk oversimplifying the complexities of van Gogh's life and the cultural environment in which he created.

Conversely, the VR project *We Are the Robots* by the artist and activist Tabor Robak seeks to address issues of cultural representation by centering the experiences of marginalized communities. This project incorporates elements of storytelling and interactive design to create a space where users can engage with the narratives of individuals from diverse backgrounds, fostering empathy and understanding.

Additionally, the game *Never Alone* (Kisima Ingitchuna) serves as a powerful example of cultural representation in VR. Developed in collaboration with the Iñupiat people of Alaska, the game incorporates traditional stories, art, and language, providing players with an authentic glimpse into Iñupiat culture. This collaborative approach not only enriches the gaming experience but also ensures that the cultural representation is respectful and accurate.

Ethical Implications and Best Practices

To promote ethical cultural representation in virtual environments, developers and creators must adopt best practices that prioritize inclusivity, respect, and collaboration. Engaging with cultural consultants and community members during the development process can help ensure that representations are accurate and meaningful. Furthermore, fostering diverse teams that reflect the cultures being represented can lead to more authentic and nuanced portrayals.

Additionally, developers should consider the potential impact of their representations on users from different cultural backgrounds. This includes being aware of how certain symbols or narratives may resonate differently across cultures and striving to create spaces that promote understanding rather than perpetuating stereotypes.

In conclusion, cultural representation in virtual environments is a multifaceted issue that requires careful consideration and ethical engagement. By grounding the discussion in theoretical frameworks, acknowledging the challenges faced by diverse communities, and learning from both positive and negative examples, we can work towards creating virtual spaces that honor and celebrate cultural diversity while fostering inclusivity and respect.

The Impact of Cultural Biases in Virtual Reality

Cultural biases in virtual reality (VR) can significantly shape user experiences and interactions within these immersive environments. As VR technology becomes increasingly prevalent, it is essential to understand how cultural representations and biases manifest and influence the way users engage with virtual worlds.

Understanding Cultural Biases

Cultural biases refer to the predispositions and stereotypes that individuals hold about different cultures, often leading to skewed perceptions and interactions. In the context of VR, these biases can be embedded in the design of virtual environments, avatars, narratives, and user interactions. Theories such as *Social Identity Theory* (Tajfel, 1979) suggest that individuals categorize themselves and others into groups, which can lead to in-group favoritism and out-group discrimination. This dynamic can be exacerbated in virtual spaces where users may feel anonymous or detached from the consequences of their actions.

Manifestations of Cultural Biases in VR

Cultural biases can manifest in several ways within VR:

- **Avatar Representation:** The design of avatars can reflect cultural stereotypes, leading to misrepresentation. For instance, avatars representing certain ethnic groups may be designed with exaggerated features that reinforce negative stereotypes, impacting how users perceive themselves and others.

- **Narrative Structures:** The stories and experiences presented in VR can often reflect a dominant cultural narrative, marginalizing alternative perspectives. For example, a VR game set in a historical context may prioritize Western narratives while neglecting indigenous viewpoints.

- **Environmental Design:** The aesthetics and cultural symbols incorporated into virtual environments can carry biases that favor certain cultures over others. A VR simulation of a city might highlight Western architecture while ignoring or misrepresenting non-Western designs.

Consequences of Cultural Biases in VR

The impact of cultural biases in VR can lead to several significant consequences:

- **Reinforcement of Stereotypes:** VR experiences that perpetuate cultural stereotypes can reinforce prejudiced views, making it more difficult for users to engage with diverse cultures in a meaningful way. This can lead to a cycle of bias where users carry these perceptions into the real world.

- **Exclusion and Alienation:** Users from underrepresented cultures may feel excluded or alienated when their identities are misrepresented or ignored in virtual environments. This can discourage participation and limit the diversity of experiences within VR.

- **Impact on Empathy:** VR has the potential to cultivate empathy by allowing users to experience life from different cultural perspectives. However, when cultural biases distort these experiences, the potential for empathy can be undermined, leading to a lack of understanding and compassion.

Examples of Cultural Bias in VR

Several examples illustrate the impact of cultural biases in VR:

- **Gaming Industry:** Many popular VR games have faced criticism for their lack of cultural sensitivity. For instance, games that feature characters from diverse backgrounds often resort to using clichéd traits that do not accurately reflect the complexity of those cultures.

- **Virtual Tours:** VR experiences designed to showcase cultural heritage can sometimes present a biased view. For example, a virtual tour of a historical site may gloss over the darker aspects of a culture's history, presenting an idealized version that fails to acknowledge historical injustices.

- **Educational VR:** In educational settings, VR applications that teach about different cultures can inadvertently reinforce biases if they rely on outdated or overly simplistic representations. For example, a VR simulation of a traditional ceremony may omit critical cultural contexts, leading to misunderstandings.

Addressing Cultural Biases in VR

To mitigate the impact of cultural biases in VR, several strategies can be employed:

- **Inclusive Design Practices:** Developers should prioritize inclusive design practices that involve representatives from diverse cultural backgrounds in the creation of VR content. This can help ensure accurate and respectful representations.

- **Cultural Sensitivity Training:** Providing cultural sensitivity training for VR developers and designers can enhance awareness of biases and promote the creation of more equitable virtual environments.

- **User Feedback Mechanisms:** Implementing mechanisms for user feedback can allow players from diverse backgrounds to voice their concerns about cultural representations, leading to improvements in future iterations of VR content.

Conclusion

The impact of cultural biases in virtual reality is a critical issue that can shape user experiences and perceptions. As VR continues to evolve, it is imperative that developers and designers remain vigilant about the cultural implications of their work. By prioritizing inclusivity and cultural sensitivity, the potential of VR to foster understanding and empathy across cultural divides can be realized, ultimately enriching the virtual experience for all users.

Bibliography

[1] Henri Tajfel, *Social Identity and Intergroup Relations*, Cambridge University Press, 1979.

Preserving Cultural Heritage in Virtual Worlds

The preservation of cultural heritage in virtual worlds has emerged as a critical concern in the age of digital technology. As virtual reality (VR) environments become increasingly sophisticated, they offer unique opportunities for the representation and safeguarding of cultural artifacts, traditions, and narratives. This section explores the theoretical frameworks, challenges, and practical examples related to the preservation of cultural heritage in virtual spaces.

Theoretical Frameworks

The preservation of cultural heritage in virtual environments can be understood through several theoretical lenses:

- **Cultural Memory Theory:** This theory posits that cultural heritage is a collective memory that shapes the identity of communities. Virtual worlds can serve as repositories of this memory, allowing users to engage with and experience cultural narratives in immersive ways.

- **Digital Anthropology:** This field examines how digital technologies affect cultural practices and interactions. It emphasizes the need for ethical considerations when representing cultures in virtual spaces, particularly regarding authenticity and representation.

- **Participatory Design:** This approach advocates for the involvement of community members in the creation and representation of their cultural heritage in virtual worlds. By engaging stakeholders, developers can ensure that virtual representations are accurate and respectful.

Challenges in Preservation

Despite the potential benefits of virtual worlds for cultural heritage preservation, several challenges must be addressed:

- **Authenticity and Representation:** One of the primary concerns is ensuring that cultural elements are represented authentically. This includes avoiding stereotypes and misrepresentations that can arise when cultures are viewed through a Western lens. For example, the depiction of Indigenous cultures in VR must be guided by those communities to prevent cultural appropriation.

- **Access and Digital Divide:** The digital divide poses a significant barrier to the preservation of cultural heritage in virtual worlds. Communities with limited access to technology may be excluded from participating in the creation and experience of their cultural narratives. This raises ethical questions about who gets to tell a culture's story.

- **Intellectual Property Rights:** The representation of cultural heritage in virtual spaces can lead to issues surrounding ownership and rights. Many traditional cultures have oral histories and practices that are not codified in ways that align with Western intellectual property laws. This can create tension between cultural expression and legal frameworks.

- **Longevity and Sustainability:** The rapid evolution of technology raises questions about the longevity of virtual representations. Cultural heritage projects may become obsolete as platforms change, leading to the potential loss of valuable cultural narratives and artifacts.

Practical Examples

Several initiatives illustrate successful efforts to preserve cultural heritage in virtual worlds:

- **The Virtual Museum of Canada:** This project allows users to explore Canadian history and culture through an interactive online platform. By collaborating with Indigenous communities, the museum ensures that cultural narratives are represented accurately and respectfully. This initiative exemplifies participatory design principles and highlights the importance of community involvement in cultural representation.

- **Google Arts & Culture:** This platform partners with museums and cultural institutions worldwide to create virtual exhibitions. Notably, the project includes the preservation of endangered languages through immersive storytelling. By providing access to cultural artifacts and narratives, Google Arts & Culture aims to foster a greater understanding and appreciation of diverse cultures.
- **The World Heritage Project:** Utilizing VR technology, this initiative seeks to digitally preserve UNESCO World Heritage Sites. By creating detailed 3D models and virtual tours, the project allows users to explore these sites while raising awareness about their significance and the threats they face from climate change and urban development.

Conclusion

The preservation of cultural heritage in virtual worlds is a multifaceted endeavor that requires careful consideration of authenticity, access, intellectual property rights, and sustainability. By employing theoretical frameworks such as cultural memory theory, digital anthropology, and participatory design, stakeholders can navigate the complexities of representing cultural narratives in virtual spaces. Successful initiatives like the Virtual Museum of Canada and Google Arts & Culture demonstrate the potential of virtual worlds to serve as platforms for cultural preservation, fostering greater understanding and appreciation of diverse heritages. As technology continues to evolve, it is imperative that ethical considerations remain at the forefront of cultural heritage preservation efforts in virtual environments.

Navigating Cultural Conflicts in Virtual Communities

In the rapidly evolving landscape of virtual reality (VR), cultural conflicts have emerged as a significant challenge within virtual communities. These conflicts can arise from diverse cultural representations, misunderstandings, and differing values among users from varied backgrounds. This section explores the complexities of navigating these cultural conflicts, drawing on relevant theories and providing illustrative examples.

Understanding Cultural Conflicts

Cultural conflicts in virtual communities can be understood through the lens of intercultural communication theory, which emphasizes the importance of context, norms, and values in interactions between individuals from different cultural backgrounds. According to Edward T. Hall's theory of high-context and low-context cultures, individuals from high-context cultures (e.g., many Asian cultures) rely heavily on implicit communication and shared experiences, while those from low-context cultures (e.g., many Western cultures) prioritize explicit communication and directness. This difference can lead to misunderstandings and conflicts in virtual interactions.

For instance, in a multiplayer online game, a player from a high-context culture may interpret a teammate's direct criticism as a personal attack, while a player from a low-context culture may view it as constructive feedback. Such misunderstandings can escalate into conflicts, affecting team dynamics and overall enjoyment of the virtual experience.

The Role of Anonymity and Avatars

Anonymity in virtual environments can exacerbate cultural conflicts. The ability to create avatars and interact without revealing one's true identity can lead to disinhibition, allowing individuals to express prejudiced views or engage in aggressive behaviors that they might avoid in real life. This phenomenon is often referred to as the "online disinhibition effect" (Suler, 2004).

For example, in virtual worlds like Second Life, users can create avatars that may not reflect their real-world identity. This freedom can lead to cultural appropriation, where individuals adopt elements of another culture without understanding or respecting their significance. Such actions can trigger backlash from members of the appropriated culture, resulting in conflicts that can escalate within virtual communities.

Examples of Cultural Conflicts

One notable example of cultural conflict in a virtual community is the backlash faced by the game developer Riot Games regarding the portrayal of characters in their game League of Legends. The game's diverse cast of characters faced criticism for cultural stereotyping and appropriation, prompting discussions about representation and respect for cultural identities. The resulting discourse highlighted the need for developers to engage with cultural consultants and communities to ensure respectful representation.

Another example is the ongoing debates within the gaming community regarding the inclusion of LGBTQ+ characters and themes. While some players advocate for greater representation, others may react negatively, leading to heated discussions and sometimes toxic environments. These conflicts often reflect broader societal issues related to acceptance and understanding of diverse identities.

Strategies for Conflict Resolution

To navigate cultural conflicts in virtual communities, several strategies can be employed:

- **Cultural Sensitivity Training:** Developers and community managers should implement training programs that educate users about cultural diversity, promoting empathy and understanding. This training can help mitigate misunderstandings and foster a more inclusive environment.

- **Facilitating Dialogue:** Creating platforms for open dialogue among users from different cultural backgrounds can help address conflicts directly. Forums, discussion boards, and moderated chats can provide spaces for users to express their concerns and seek common ground.

- **Inclusive Design Practices:** Game developers should prioritize inclusive design practices that consider diverse cultural perspectives. Involving cultural consultants during the development process can help ensure that representations are respectful and accurate.

- **Community Guidelines:** Establishing clear community guidelines that promote respectful interactions and outline consequences for discriminatory behavior can help create a safer environment for all users.

Conclusion

Navigating cultural conflicts in virtual communities is a complex but essential endeavor. By understanding the underlying theories of intercultural communication, recognizing the role of anonymity and avatars, and implementing effective strategies for conflict resolution, virtual communities can foster a more inclusive and respectful environment. As virtual reality continues to grow, addressing cultural conflicts will be crucial in ensuring that these spaces are welcoming for users from all backgrounds.

Bibliography

[1] Suler, J. (2004). The Online Disinhibition Effect. *CyberPsychology & Behavior*, 7(3), 321-326.

Exploring Intercultural Communication in Virtual Reality

Intercultural communication is a pivotal aspect of human interaction, and in the context of virtual reality (VR), it takes on new dimensions. As users from diverse backgrounds engage in shared virtual spaces, the dynamics of communication evolve, influenced by cultural norms, values, and technological affordances. This section delves into the theoretical frameworks, challenges, and practical examples related to intercultural communication within VR environments.

Theoretical Frameworks

Several theories provide a foundation for understanding intercultural communication in VR. One prominent framework is **Edward T. Hall's High-Context and Low-Context Cultures.** Hall posits that cultures can be categorized based on their communication styles. High-context cultures (e.g., Japan, China) rely heavily on implicit messages and non-verbal cues, while low-context cultures (e.g., the United States, Germany) favor explicit verbal communication. In VR, where avatars and visual cues are central, these differences can lead to misunderstandings.

Another relevant theory is **Geert Hofstede's Cultural Dimensions Theory**, which identifies key dimensions of culture that influence communication styles, including:

- **Power Distance Index (PDI):** The extent to which less powerful members of a society defer to more powerful members.

- **Individualism vs. Collectivism (IDV):** The degree to which individuals are integrated into groups.

- **Uncertainty Avoidance Index (UAI):** A culture's tolerance for ambiguity and uncertainty.

- **Masculinity vs. Femininity (MAS):** The distribution of emotional roles between the genders.

Understanding these dimensions can help VR developers create more culturally sensitive environments that accommodate diverse communication styles.

Challenges in Intercultural Communication in VR

Despite the potential for enhanced communication, several challenges impede effective intercultural exchanges in virtual environments:

- **Language Barriers:** While many VR platforms support multiple languages, nuances in language can lead to misinterpretations. For instance, idiomatic expressions may not translate well, causing confusion among users from different linguistic backgrounds.

- **Cultural Misinterpretations:** Users may misinterpret gestures, facial expressions, or avatar behaviors based on their cultural backgrounds. For example, direct eye contact is considered a sign of confidence in some cultures, while in others, it may be perceived as disrespectful.

- **Stereotyping and Bias:** Pre-existing stereotypes can influence interactions in VR. Users may project their biases onto avatars, leading to discriminatory behavior or exclusionary practices.

- **Technological Limitations:** The fidelity of avatars and virtual environments can affect communication. Low-quality graphics may hinder the ability to convey emotions effectively, while lag or technical glitches can disrupt conversations.

Practical Examples of Intercultural Communication in VR

Several VR platforms and experiences illustrate the complexities of intercultural communication:

BIBLIOGRAPHY

- **VRChat**: This popular social VR platform allows users to create and customize avatars, engage in conversations, and participate in virtual events. However, users often report instances of cultural misunderstandings due to varying communication styles. For example, a user from a collectivist culture may perceive a direct, assertive approach as rude, while a user from an individualistic culture may see it as a sign of confidence.

- **AltspaceVR**: This platform hosts events and meetups, bringing together users from diverse backgrounds. Facilitators often implement guidelines for respectful communication, emphasizing the importance of cultural sensitivity. However, challenges remain, such as users unintentionally using culturally inappropriate humor, which can alienate others.

- **Immersive Language Learning Applications**: Several VR applications aim to teach languages through immersive experiences. For instance, users can practice conversational skills in realistic scenarios. However, the effectiveness of these applications hinges on the ability to navigate cultural nuances, such as understanding local customs or etiquette.

Strategies for Enhancing Intercultural Communication in VR

To mitigate the challenges of intercultural communication in VR, several strategies can be implemented:

- **Cultural Training Programs**: Developers and community managers can offer training sessions to educate users about cultural differences and communication styles. This can foster a more inclusive environment and reduce misunderstandings.

- **Customizable Communication Settings**: VR platforms can allow users to customize their communication preferences, such as selecting cultural norms they wish to adhere to during interactions. This feature can help bridge gaps between high-context and low-context communicators.

- **Feedback Mechanisms**: Implementing feedback systems can enable users to report misunderstandings or inappropriate behavior. This feedback can inform developers about potential cultural issues and guide improvements.

- **Promoting Empathy through Immersive Experiences**: VR has the unique ability to foster empathy by allowing users to experience life from another person's perspective. This can be particularly powerful in understanding cultural challenges and promoting cross-cultural understanding.

Conclusion

As virtual reality continues to evolve, the importance of intercultural communication becomes increasingly salient. By understanding the theoretical frameworks that underpin cultural interactions, recognizing the challenges that arise, and implementing strategies to enhance communication, VR can serve as a powerful tool for fostering intercultural dialogue. In doing so, we can create virtual environments that not only reflect our diverse world but also promote understanding, empathy, and collaboration among users from all walks of life.

Cultural Appropriation in Virtual Environments

Cultural appropriation is a complex and often contentious issue that arises in various contexts, including virtual environments. It refers to the adoption of elements from one culture by members of another culture, particularly when the appropriating culture is in a position of power or privilege. In virtual reality (VR) and augmented reality (AR) settings, where users can create and manipulate digital representations of cultures, the implications of cultural appropriation become particularly nuanced. This section explores the theoretical frameworks surrounding cultural appropriation, the problems it presents in virtual environments, and relevant examples that illustrate these challenges.

Theoretical Frameworks

The concept of cultural appropriation is often discussed within the broader context of postcolonial theory, which examines the power dynamics between colonizers and the colonized. Edward Said's notion of *Orientalism* (1978) highlights how Western representations of Eastern cultures often distort and stereotype the original cultures for entertainment or profit. This framework can be applied to virtual environments, where developers and users may create content that misrepresents or oversimplifies cultural elements.

Another relevant theory is that of *cultural hegemony*, as described by Antonio Gramsci. This theory posits that dominant cultures impose their values and norms on subordinate cultures, which can lead to the commodification of cultural practices. In VR, this can manifest as the commercialization of cultural symbols without proper acknowledgment or respect for their significance.

Problems of Cultural Appropriation in Virtual Reality

Cultural appropriation in virtual environments raises several ethical concerns:

- **Misrepresentation and Stereotyping:** Virtual representations of cultures can perpetuate stereotypes and inaccuracies, leading to a distorted understanding of the appropriated culture. For example, a game that features a fictionalized version of Indigenous cultures may simplify complex traditions into caricatures, undermining the richness of those cultures.

- **Lack of Consent:** Cultural elements are often appropriated without the consent of the originating community. This raises questions about ownership and the rights of individuals to control their cultural expressions. In VR, users may create avatars or environments that incorporate sacred symbols or traditional attire without understanding their significance.

- **Economic Exploitation:** When cultural elements are used for profit by individuals or companies outside the originating culture, it can result in economic exploitation. For instance, a VR game that sells in-game items inspired by Indigenous art may profit from those designs while the original artists receive no compensation or recognition.

- **Erasure of Cultural Context:** In virtual spaces, cultural symbols may be stripped of their context, leading to an erasure of meaning. This can diminish the importance of cultural practices and reduce them to mere aesthetics. For example, a virtual reality environment featuring traditional African masks may present them as decorative items rather than as objects with deep cultural significance.

Examples of Cultural Appropriation in Virtual Reality

Several high-profile cases illustrate the challenges of cultural appropriation in virtual environments:

- **Video Games:** Many video games have faced backlash for appropriating cultural elements without proper representation. For instance, the game *Overwatch* received criticism for its portrayal of characters inspired by various cultures, with some arguing that the designs were superficial and failed to accurately represent the cultures they drew from.

- **Virtual Reality Experiences:** Immersive experiences that claim to offer cultural education can inadvertently perpetuate appropriation. For example, a VR experience that allows users to explore a simulated version of a sacred site may do so without the involvement or permission of the community that holds that site sacred.

- **Social Media and User-Generated Content:** Platforms that allow users to create and share virtual content can amplify issues of cultural appropriation. Users may create avatars or environments that incorporate elements from marginalized cultures, often without understanding the implications of their actions. This can lead to a cycle of appropriation that is difficult to regulate.

Ethical Considerations and Best Practices

To navigate the complexities of cultural appropriation in virtual environments, several ethical considerations and best practices can be adopted:

- **Engagement with Cultural Communities:** Developers and users should engage with the communities whose cultures they wish to represent. This can include seeking permission, collaborating with cultural representatives, and ensuring that cultural elements are portrayed accurately and respectfully.

- **Education and Awareness:** Raising awareness about cultural appropriation and its implications is crucial. This can involve providing resources and training for developers and users to understand the cultural significance of the elements they wish to incorporate into their virtual spaces.

- **Promoting Authentic Representation:** Encouraging authentic representation of cultures in virtual environments can help mitigate appropriation. This can include featuring creators from the cultures being represented and ensuring that their voices are heard in the development process.

- **Establishing Guidelines:** Platforms and developers can establish guidelines for cultural representation in virtual environments. These guidelines can outline best practices for respectful engagement with cultural elements and provide a framework for addressing instances of appropriation.

In conclusion, cultural appropriation in virtual environments presents significant ethical challenges that require careful consideration. By engaging with cultural communities, promoting authentic representation, and raising awareness about the implications of appropriation, we can work towards creating virtual spaces that respect and honor the diverse cultures they draw from. The responsibility lies with both developers and users to ensure that virtual realities do not become platforms for exploitation but rather spaces for cultural exchange and understanding.

Promoting Cultural Exchange and Understanding

In the rapidly evolving landscape of virtual reality (VR), the potential for cultural exchange and understanding is unprecedented. Virtual environments serve as platforms where individuals from diverse backgrounds can interact, share experiences, and learn from one another. This section explores how VR can facilitate cultural exchange, the challenges involved, and practical examples that highlight its effectiveness.

Theoretical Framework

Cultural exchange in VR can be analyzed through the lens of intercultural communication theory, which emphasizes the importance of context, perception, and interaction in understanding cultural differences. According to Gudykunst's Anxiety/Uncertainty Management (AUM) theory, effective communication across cultures requires managing anxiety and uncertainty, which can be achieved through immersive experiences that foster empathy and understanding [1].

Additionally, the Social Identity Theory posits that individuals derive a sense of self from their group memberships, which can be expanded in virtual environments. By embodying avatars that represent different cultures, users can experience and understand cultural identities beyond their own, promoting a sense of global citizenship [2].

Mechanisms for Cultural Exchange

- **Immersive Experiences:** VR allows users to immerse themselves in different cultural settings, such as participating in traditional ceremonies or exploring historical landmarks. These experiences can lead to increased cultural awareness and appreciation.

- **Collaborative Projects:** Virtual platforms can host collaborative projects where individuals from various cultures work together to create art, music, or educational content. This collaboration fosters dialogue and understanding.

- **Cultural Simulations:** Developers can create simulations that reflect the customs, values, and social norms of different cultures. Users can navigate these simulations to learn about cultural practices in a safe and engaging environment.

Challenges to Cultural Exchange

Despite the potential benefits, several challenges hinder effective cultural exchange in VR:

- **Cultural Misrepresentation:** The risk of cultural stereotypes and misrepresentation in VR content can lead to misunderstanding rather than fostering appreciation. Developers must engage with cultural experts to create authentic representations.

- **Digital Divide:** Access to VR technology is not uniform across the globe. Socioeconomic barriers can prevent marginalized communities from participating in cultural exchange, thereby perpetuating existing inequalities.

- **Language Barriers:** While VR can transcend physical boundaries, language differences can still pose significant challenges. Effective communication tools and multilingual support are essential for meaningful interaction.

Case Studies

Several initiatives illustrate the potential of VR to promote cultural exchange:

- **The Virtual Reality Cultural Exchange (VRCE):** This project connects schools from different countries through VR technology. Students participate in virtual field trips, share cultural presentations, and engage in discussions, thereby enhancing their understanding of global perspectives.

- **Cultural Heritage Preservation Projects:** Organizations such as UNESCO have utilized VR to create immersive experiences of endangered cultural sites. Users can explore these sites virtually, raising awareness and appreciation for global heritage.

- **Social VR Platforms:** Platforms like *AltspaceVR* and *VRChat* allow users to create and join cultural events, such as international festivals or art exhibitions. These spaces encourage users to share their cultural practices and learn from others in real-time.

Conclusion

Promoting cultural exchange and understanding through virtual reality is not without its challenges, but the potential benefits are immense. By leveraging the immersive nature of VR, we can foster empathy, break down cultural barriers, and create a more interconnected world. As we continue to develop and refine VR technologies, it is crucial to prioritize ethical considerations and inclusivity to ensure that cultural exchange is genuine and enriching for all participants.

Bibliography

[1] Gudykunst, W. B. (2005). *Anxiety/Uncertainty Management Theory.* In W. B. Gudykunst (Ed.), *Theorizing about Intercultural Communication* (pp. 143-176). Sage Publications.

[2] Tajfel, H. (1979). *Individuals and Groups in Social Psychology.* British Journal of Social and Clinical Psychology, 18(2), 183-190.

The Potential for Virtual Reality to Bridge Cultural Divides

Virtual reality (VR) holds significant promise as a tool for bridging cultural divides, offering immersive experiences that can foster understanding and empathy among diverse groups. By enabling users to step into the shoes of others, VR can challenge preconceived notions and stereotypes, facilitating cross-cultural dialogue in ways that traditional media cannot. This section explores the theoretical frameworks, practical applications, and challenges associated with using VR to bridge cultural divides.

Theoretical Frameworks

The potential of VR to bridge cultural divides can be understood through several theoretical lenses, including social presence theory, empathy theory, and constructivist learning theory.

Social Presence Theory Social presence theory posits that the degree of salience of the other person in a mediated communication influences the quality of interaction. In VR, users experience a heightened sense of presence, making interactions feel more genuine and impactful. This immersive quality can enhance the ability to connect with individuals from different cultural backgrounds, leading to deeper understanding and reduced bias.

Empathy Theory   Empathy theory suggests that experiencing another person's perspective can foster emotional connections and understanding. VR experiences, such as those that allow users to embody individuals from different cultures, can evoke strong empathetic responses. For instance, VR simulations that depict the experiences of refugees or marginalized communities can help users grasp the complexities of their challenges, potentially leading to increased compassion and advocacy.

Constructivist Learning Theory   Constructivist learning theory emphasizes the importance of experiential learning in knowledge acquisition. VR provides a unique platform for experiential learning, allowing users to engage with diverse cultures in an interactive manner. By participating in cultural rituals, traditions, or historical events through VR, users can construct knowledge that transcends traditional educational boundaries.

Practical Applications

Numerous initiatives and projects have emerged that leverage VR to bridge cultural divides:

1. **Virtual Cultural Exchanges**   Programs such as *VR for Good* and *Google Arts & Culture* facilitate virtual cultural exchanges, allowing users to explore different cultures from their homes. These platforms offer guided tours of cultural landmarks, interactive storytelling experiences, and opportunities to engage with local communities through VR, fostering mutual understanding.

2. **Empathy-Building Experiences**   Organizations like *The United Nations* and *The Refugee Project* have developed VR experiences that immerse users in the lives of individuals facing adversity. For example, *Clouds Over Sidra* is a VR film that places viewers in a Syrian refugee camp, enabling them to witness the daily struggles and resilience of its inhabitants. Such experiences can be instrumental in humanizing complex issues and promoting empathy.

3. **Educational Initiatives**   Educational institutions are increasingly incorporating VR into their curricula to promote cultural awareness. Programs that utilize VR simulations to teach students about different cultural practices, histories, and languages can enhance understanding and appreciation of diversity. For instance, VR-based language learning platforms allow students to engage with native speakers in realistic scenarios, breaking down cultural barriers.

Challenges and Considerations

While the potential of VR to bridge cultural divides is promising, several challenges must be addressed:

1. **Accessibility** Access to VR technology remains a significant barrier. Socioeconomic disparities can limit the availability of VR experiences to privileged groups, potentially exacerbating existing cultural divides. Ensuring equitable access to VR technology is crucial for its effectiveness as a bridging tool.

2. **Cultural Sensitivity** Developing VR content that accurately represents diverse cultures is essential. Misrepresentation or oversimplification of cultural practices can lead to further misunderstanding and reinforce stereotypes. Collaborating with cultural representatives during the development process can help mitigate these risks.

3. **Psychological Impact** Immersive experiences can have profound psychological effects on users. While empathy-building experiences can foster understanding, they may also evoke discomfort or distress. It is essential to provide appropriate context and support for users engaging with challenging content.

Conclusion

In conclusion, virtual reality has the potential to serve as a powerful tool for bridging cultural divides by fostering empathy, understanding, and collaboration. By leveraging theoretical frameworks that emphasize social presence, empathy, and experiential learning, VR can create meaningful connections between individuals from diverse backgrounds. However, addressing challenges related to accessibility, cultural sensitivity, and psychological impact is vital to ensure that VR serves as a constructive force for cultural exchange. As the technology continues to evolve, its role in promoting cross-cultural understanding will undoubtedly grow, offering new opportunities for dialogue and collaboration in an increasingly interconnected world.

Ethical Considerations in Developing Culturally Sensitive Virtual Reality

The development of virtual reality (VR) technologies presents unique ethical challenges, particularly regarding cultural sensitivity. As VR becomes increasingly integrated into various aspects of life, from entertainment to education, the need for culturally sensitive design is paramount. This section explores the ethical considerations involved in creating culturally aware virtual environments, drawing on relevant theories, identifying potential problems, and providing illustrative examples.

Understanding Cultural Sensitivity in VR

Cultural sensitivity in VR can be defined as the awareness and respect for the diverse cultural backgrounds of users, which informs the design and content of virtual experiences. This concept is grounded in the broader framework of cultural competence, which emphasizes understanding, valuing, and responding to the cultural differences of individuals and communities. According to [?], cultural competence involves a continuous process of learning and adapting, which is essential for developers and designers in the VR space.

Theoretical Frameworks

Several theoretical frameworks can guide the development of culturally sensitive VR. One prominent theory is Edward Said's concept of *Orientalism*, which critiques the Western portrayal of Eastern cultures as exotic and inferior. Applying this framework to VR design entails avoiding stereotypes and ensuring authentic representation of diverse cultures. Additionally, the *Social Identity Theory* [2] highlights how individuals derive a sense of self from their group memberships. This theory underscores the importance of accurately representing cultural identities in VR to foster a sense of belonging and validation among users.

Challenges in Culturally Sensitive VR Development

Despite the importance of cultural sensitivity, several challenges complicate its implementation in VR:

- **Cultural Appropriation:** Developers may inadvertently appropriate cultural elements without understanding their significance. This can lead to the commodification of culture, which often results in backlash from the communities represented. For instance, a VR game that uses indigenous symbols as mere aesthetic features can be seen as disrespectful.

- **Representation and Stereotyping:** Inaccurate or stereotypical representations can perpetuate harmful narratives. For example, a VR experience that portrays a culture solely through the lens of poverty or violence fails to capture the richness and diversity of that culture.

- **Access and Inclusivity:** Not all cultural groups have equal access to VR technologies. The digital divide can exacerbate existing inequalities, making it essential for developers to consider accessibility in their designs.

Ethical Guidelines for Culturally Sensitive VR Development

To address these challenges, developers should adhere to several ethical guidelines:

1. **Engagement with Cultural Representatives:** Collaborating with cultural experts and community members during the development process ensures that representations are accurate and respectful. This engagement can take the form of focus groups, consultations, or partnerships with cultural organizations.

2. **Inclusive Design Practices:** Incorporating inclusive design principles allows for diverse user experiences. This includes considering various cultural perspectives in storytelling, aesthetics, and interaction methods.

3. **Transparency and Education:** Providing users with context about the cultural elements represented in VR can enhance understanding and appreciation. Developers should include educational resources that explain the significance of cultural symbols and practices.

Examples of Culturally Sensitive VR Applications

Several VR applications exemplify culturally sensitive practices:

- **The Virtual Reality Museum of Canada:** This platform showcases indigenous cultures through immersive experiences that highlight their histories and traditions. Collaborating with indigenous communities ensures authentic representation and promotes cultural preservation.

- **Google's Arts and Culture:** This initiative allows users to explore cultural heritage sites and artifacts from around the world. By providing detailed information about the cultural significance of each site, it fosters respect and understanding among users.

- **The VR experience "The Night Cafe":** Based on Vincent van Gogh's paintings, this immersive environment invites users to interact with the artist's world. By focusing on the emotional and historical context of the artworks, it transcends mere visual representation and fosters a deeper connection to the culture of the time.

Conclusion

In conclusion, developing culturally sensitive virtual reality requires a nuanced understanding of cultural dynamics and a commitment to ethical practices. By engaging with cultural representatives, adhering to inclusive design principles, and educating users about cultural contexts, developers can create VR experiences that respect and celebrate diversity. As VR continues to evolve, prioritizing cultural sensitivity will be essential in fostering a more inclusive digital landscape.

Protecting Indigenous Knowledge and Cultural Rights in Virtual Spaces

In the age of virtual reality (VR), the protection of Indigenous knowledge and cultural rights has emerged as a critical issue. As virtual environments become increasingly popular for cultural expression, education, and commerce, it is vital to ensure that Indigenous peoples retain control over their cultural heritage and knowledge. This section explores the theoretical frameworks, challenges, and examples associated with protecting Indigenous knowledge within virtual spaces.

Theoretical Frameworks

The protection of Indigenous knowledge can be understood through several theoretical lenses, including cultural sovereignty, intellectual property rights, and digital ethics.

Cultural Sovereignty Cultural sovereignty refers to the right of Indigenous peoples to maintain and control their cultural practices, languages, and traditions. This concept emphasizes the importance of self-determination and the ability to define one's cultural identity without external interference. In virtual spaces, cultural sovereignty is often challenged by the commodification of Indigenous cultures, where elements of their heritage are appropriated without consent.

Intellectual Property Rights Intellectual property (IP) rights provide a legal framework for protecting creative works, inventions, and symbols. However, traditional IP laws are often inadequate for safeguarding Indigenous knowledge, which is typically communal and passed down through generations. The application of Western IP frameworks can lead to the misappropriation of Indigenous cultural expressions, as seen in cases where traditional designs are trademarked by non-Indigenous entities.

Digital Ethics Digital ethics examines the moral implications of technology use, including issues of consent, representation, and equity. In the context of virtual spaces, ethical considerations must address how Indigenous knowledge is represented and who has the right to access and share this information.

Challenges in Protecting Indigenous Knowledge

Despite the potential benefits of virtual reality for cultural expression, several challenges hinder the protection of Indigenous knowledge:

Misappropriation and Exploitation One of the most significant challenges is the risk of misappropriation, where non-Indigenous individuals or corporations exploit Indigenous cultural elements for profit. This exploitation often occurs without any benefit to the Indigenous communities themselves. For instance, virtual worlds may feature Indigenous-inspired avatars, clothing, or artifacts, which can dilute the significance of these cultural elements.

Lack of Representation Indigenous peoples are often underrepresented in the development of virtual reality technologies. This lack of representation can lead to the creation of virtual spaces that do not accurately reflect Indigenous cultures or values. As a result, the narratives and experiences of Indigenous peoples may be misrepresented or ignored entirely.

Digital Divide The digital divide remains a significant barrier for many Indigenous communities, limiting their access to the technologies required to participate in virtual spaces. This divide can exacerbate existing inequalities and hinder Indigenous peoples' ability to protect and promote their cultural heritage in digital environments.

Examples of Protection Strategies

Several strategies have been proposed or implemented to protect Indigenous knowledge and cultural rights in virtual spaces:

Community-Controlled Platforms Creating community-controlled virtual platforms allows Indigenous peoples to curate their cultural content and narratives actively. For example, platforms like *IndigenousX* provide a space for Indigenous voices to share their stories, ensuring that cultural knowledge is disseminated accurately and ethically.

Collaborative Design Processes Engaging Indigenous communities in the design and development of virtual reality experiences is essential. Collaborative approaches can ensure that cultural representations are authentic and respectful. For instance, the *Virtual Reality Indigenous Heritage Project* seeks to involve Indigenous communities in creating immersive experiences that honor their cultural heritage.

Legal Frameworks and Policies Establishing legal frameworks that recognize and protect Indigenous knowledge in virtual environments is crucial. This can include adapting existing IP laws to better serve Indigenous communities or developing new policies that address the unique aspects of Indigenous cultural heritage. For example, the *Nagoya Protocol* on Access and Benefit-sharing provides a framework for ensuring that Indigenous peoples benefit from the use of their traditional knowledge.

Conclusion

Protecting Indigenous knowledge and cultural rights in virtual spaces is a complex and multifaceted issue that requires a collaborative and ethical approach. By prioritizing cultural sovereignty, adapting legal frameworks, and ensuring representation in virtual reality development, we can create environments that respect and honor Indigenous cultures. As virtual reality continues to evolve, it is imperative that Indigenous peoples are empowered to control their cultural narratives and protect their knowledge from exploitation and misappropriation.

Chapter Four: Virtual Reality and Human Rights

Equal Access to Virtual Reality

The Digital Divide and Virtual Reality

The concept of the digital divide refers to the gap between individuals who have easy access to digital technology and those who do not. This divide is particularly pronounced in the context of Virtual Reality (VR), where access to technology can significantly influence participation in VR environments and experiences. The digital divide can be analyzed through various lenses, including socioeconomic status, geographic location, education, and age.

Understanding the Digital Divide

The digital divide encompasses several dimensions, including:

- **Access:** The availability of devices, internet connectivity, and VR technology.

- **Skills:** The ability to use technology effectively, including understanding how to navigate VR environments.

- **Content:** The relevance and availability of VR content that caters to diverse interests and needs.

As the VR industry continues to grow, the implications of the digital divide become increasingly significant. For instance, a study by the Pew Research Center found that 15% of Americans do not have high-speed internet access, which directly impacts their ability to engage with VR platforms that require substantial bandwidth for optimal performance [?].

Socioeconomic Barriers

Socioeconomic factors play a crucial role in determining access to VR technology. Individuals from lower-income backgrounds may struggle to afford the necessary hardware, such as VR headsets and high-performance computers. For example, the Oculus Quest 2, a popular VR headset, retails for around $299, not including the cost of a compatible computer or gaming console. This financial barrier limits access for many potential users, particularly in underprivileged communities.

Moreover, socioeconomic status often correlates with educational opportunities. Individuals with limited access to education may lack the technical skills required to navigate VR environments effectively. This creates a cycle where those who are already disadvantaged remain excluded from emerging technologies and experiences.

Geographic Disparities

Geographic location significantly influences access to VR technology. Urban areas tend to have better infrastructure, including high-speed internet and technology hubs, compared to rural areas. This disparity can lead to a concentration of VR experiences in urban centers, leaving rural populations with limited access. For instance, a report by the Federal Communications Commission (FCC) highlighted that rural Americans are more likely to lack access to broadband internet compared to their urban counterparts, further exacerbating the digital divide in the context of VR [?].

Age and Technological Proficiency

Age is another factor that contributes to the digital divide. Older adults may be less familiar with technology and, consequently, less likely to adopt VR. A survey conducted by AARP found that only 10% of adults aged 50 and older have tried VR, compared to 30% of younger adults aged 18-29 [?]. This generational gap in technology adoption can hinder the development of VR content that caters to older audiences, further entrenching the divide.

Implications for Virtual Reality Experiences

The digital divide has significant implications for the development and accessibility of VR experiences. If certain demographics are systematically excluded from VR technology, the resulting virtual environments may lack diversity and representation. This can lead to a homogenization of experiences that do not reflect the richness of different cultures and perspectives.

Furthermore, the digital divide can perpetuate existing inequalities in society. For example, VR has the potential to serve as a powerful educational tool, offering immersive learning experiences. However, if access to these resources is limited to specific groups, the educational benefits of VR will not be equitably distributed.

Bridging the Digital Divide

Addressing the digital divide in VR requires a multi-faceted approach. Potential solutions include:

- **Subsidizing Technology:** Governments and organizations can provide subsidies for VR hardware to low-income individuals and communities.

- **Expanding Internet Access:** Initiatives to improve broadband infrastructure in rural and underserved areas are essential for increasing access to VR.

- **Educational Programs:** Offering training programs that focus on VR technology and digital literacy can empower individuals to engage with VR effectively.

- **Inclusive Content Creation:** Developers should prioritize creating diverse and culturally relevant VR content that appeals to a wide range of users.

In conclusion, the digital divide presents significant challenges for the equitable distribution of Virtual Reality experiences. As VR technology continues to evolve, it is crucial to address these disparities to ensure that all individuals, regardless of their background, have the opportunity to participate in and benefit from the immersive experiences that VR has to offer.

Accessibility for People with Disabilities in Virtual Worlds

The advent of virtual reality (VR) technology has opened up new avenues for interaction, education, and entertainment. However, the potential benefits of VR can only be realized if these environments are accessible to all users, including individuals with disabilities. Accessibility in virtual worlds is not merely a technical requirement; it is a fundamental aspect of human rights and social inclusion. This section explores the theoretical frameworks, existing challenges, and practical examples related to making virtual reality accessible for people with disabilities.

Theoretical Frameworks

Accessibility in virtual environments can be understood through various theoretical lenses, including the Social Model of Disability and Universal Design. The Social Model of Disability posits that disability is not an inherent attribute of an individual but rather a consequence of societal barriers. This perspective emphasizes the need to create environments that accommodate diverse needs, thus enabling full participation in virtual worlds.

Universal Design, on the other hand, advocates for the creation of products and environments that are usable by all people, to the greatest extent possible, without the need for adaptation. This principle can be applied to VR development to ensure that virtual experiences are inclusive from the outset.

Challenges to Accessibility

Despite the theoretical frameworks supporting accessibility, several challenges persist in virtual reality environments:

- **Physical Limitations:** Many VR systems require physical movement, which can be a barrier for individuals with mobility impairments. For instance, traditional VR setups often necessitate standing or walking, which may not be feasible for everyone.

- **Sensory Disabilities:** Users with visual or auditory impairments may find it difficult to navigate VR environments that rely heavily on visual or auditory cues. For example, a VR game that utilizes sound to indicate danger may leave a deaf player unaware of impending threats.

- **Cognitive Disabilities:** Complex interfaces and fast-paced environments can be overwhelming for individuals with cognitive disabilities, making it challenging to engage with VR content effectively.

- **Lack of Standards:** There is currently no universal standard for accessibility in VR, leading to inconsistencies in how different platforms address the needs of users with disabilities. This lack of regulation can result in experiences that are either inaccessible or poorly designed.

Examples of Accessible Virtual Reality

Despite these challenges, there are notable examples of VR applications that prioritize accessibility:

- **Accessible Gaming:** Games like *Half + Half* incorporate features such as customizable controls and visual aids to accommodate players with various disabilities. This game allows players to adjust their avatars and gameplay mechanics to suit their individual needs.

- **Educational Platforms:** Platforms like *Engage* provide immersive learning experiences while incorporating accessibility features such as text-to-speech and customizable environments. These features enable learners with disabilities to participate fully in virtual classrooms.

- **Social VR:** Applications like *AltspaceVR* have made strides in creating inclusive social spaces by offering options for closed captioning, sign language interpretation, and customizable avatars that represent diverse identities and abilities.

Strategies for Improvement

To enhance accessibility in virtual reality, developers and stakeholders can adopt several strategies:

- **User-Centered Design:** Involving users with disabilities in the design process can provide valuable insights into their needs and preferences, leading to more effective solutions.

- **Flexible Controls:** Providing multiple input methods (e.g., voice commands, adaptive controllers) can help accommodate users with varying physical abilities.

- **Clear Communication:** Ensuring that instructions and feedback are conveyed through multiple modalities (e.g., visual, auditory, and haptic) can help users with sensory disabilities navigate virtual environments more easily.

- **Testing and Feedback:** Regular testing with diverse user groups can identify accessibility issues and inform ongoing improvements. Developers should seek feedback from individuals with disabilities to ensure that their experiences are as seamless as possible.

Conclusion

In conclusion, the accessibility of virtual reality for people with disabilities is a critical issue that requires immediate attention. By embracing theoretical frameworks such as the Social Model of Disability and Universal Design, addressing existing challenges, and implementing effective strategies, we can create virtual worlds that are inclusive and empowering for all users. As VR technology continues to evolve, it is imperative that accessibility remains a priority, ensuring that no one is left behind in the immersive experiences that virtual reality has to offer.

Socioeconomic Barriers to Virtual Reality Adoption

The adoption of Virtual Reality (VR) technology has been heralded as a transformative leap in how individuals interact with digital environments. However, this leap is not universally accessible. Socioeconomic barriers significantly impede the widespread adoption of VR, creating a digital divide that mirrors existing inequalities in society. This section explores the various socioeconomic factors that contribute to these barriers, highlighting the implications for equity and inclusion in virtual environments.

Understanding Socioeconomic Barriers

Socioeconomic status (SES) encompasses a range of factors, including income, education, occupation, and social class. These factors collectively influence an individual's access to technology, including VR systems. The disparity in access is often referred to as the "digital divide," a term that captures the gap between those who can afford and utilize technology and those who cannot.

Financial Barriers

The cost of VR hardware and software remains a significant barrier to adoption. High-quality VR systems, such as the Oculus Rift, HTC Vive, and Valve Index, can range from $400 to over $1,000, excluding the cost of a compatible computer, which may also require substantial investment. For many low-income households, these costs are prohibitive.

$$\text{Total Cost} = \text{Cost of VR Headset} + \text{Cost of Compatible Computer} \quad (11)$$

For example, a basic setup might require an investment of around $1,500, a figure that exceeds the monthly income of many families living below the poverty line. This financial barrier creates a situation where VR technology is predominantly accessible to wealthier individuals, further entrenching existing inequalities.

Educational Barriers

Education plays a crucial role in technology adoption. Individuals with higher levels of education are more likely to understand and utilize new technologies effectively. A lack of familiarity with technology can deter individuals from engaging with VR, as they may perceive it as complex or unnecessary.

Moreover, educational institutions in lower socioeconomic areas may lack the resources to provide students with exposure to VR technology. Schools in affluent neighborhoods often have the budget to invest in cutting-edge technology, while those in economically disadvantaged areas struggle to provide basic educational resources. This disparity in access to technology education perpetuates a cycle of inequality.

Occupational Barriers

The type of occupation also influences access to VR. Professionals in tech-savvy industries, such as gaming, design, and engineering, are more likely to encounter and utilize VR technology in their work. In contrast, individuals in lower-wage jobs may not have the opportunity to experience VR, either in the workplace or in their personal lives.

This occupational divide can lead to a lack of awareness and understanding of VR's potential benefits, further limiting its adoption among lower socioeconomic groups. The disparity in occupational exposure creates a knowledge gap that is difficult to bridge without targeted educational initiatives.

Geographical Barriers

Geography plays a significant role in the adoption of VR technology. Urban areas typically have better access to high-speed internet, technology retailers, and VR experiences than rural areas. For instance, a study by the Pew Research Center found that 73% of urban residents have access to high-speed internet, compared to only 63% of rural residents.

This geographical disparity can limit the ability of individuals in rural areas to explore and adopt VR technologies. Additionally, VR experiences, such as gaming centers or VR arcades, are often concentrated in urban locations, making it challenging for rural residents to engage with VR.

Cultural Barriers

Cultural perceptions of technology can also impact VR adoption. In some communities, there may be skepticism or resistance to new technologies due to cultural beliefs or past experiences with technology. For example, individuals from cultures that prioritize face-to-face interactions may view VR as a barrier to genuine social engagement.

Moreover, the representation of diverse cultures within VR content is often lacking. If individuals do not see themselves reflected in the virtual experiences available, they may feel alienated from the technology. This lack of representation can deter potential users from adopting VR, further exacerbating the socioeconomic divide.

Addressing Socioeconomic Barriers

To promote equitable access to VR technology, several strategies can be implemented:

1. **Subsidized Programs:** Governments and organizations can develop programs to subsidize the cost of VR hardware and software for low-income individuals. This could include partnerships with technology companies to provide discounts or grants for educational institutions.

2. **Educational Initiatives:** Schools and community organizations can implement programs to educate individuals about VR technology, its applications, and its benefits. Providing hands-on experiences in schools can demystify the technology and encourage interest.

3. **Mobile VR Units:** Deploying mobile VR units to underserved communities can provide access to VR experiences without the need for individuals to invest in expensive equipment. These units can offer immersive educational experiences, gaming, and other applications.

4. **Culturally Relevant Content:** Developers should prioritize creating VR content that reflects diverse cultures and experiences. By ensuring representation, individuals from various backgrounds may feel more inclined to engage with the technology.

Conclusion

Socioeconomic barriers to VR adoption present significant challenges to achieving equity in access to technology. Financial, educational, occupational, geographical, and cultural factors all contribute to a landscape where VR remains an exclusive experience for many. By recognizing and addressing these barriers, stakeholders can work towards a more inclusive virtual reality landscape that benefits individuals from all socioeconomic backgrounds. The future of VR should not be a reflection of existing inequalities but rather a platform for bridging divides and fostering understanding across diverse communities.

Ensuring Privacy and Data Protection in Virtual Environments

As virtual reality (VR) continues to proliferate across various sectors, the pressing concern of privacy and data protection in these immersive environments has become increasingly salient. Users often share personal information, preferences, and behaviors while engaging in virtual worlds, raising significant ethical and legal questions about how this data is collected, used, and protected. This section delves into the theoretical frameworks surrounding privacy in virtual environments, the challenges faced, and concrete examples illustrating the implications of data mishandling.

Theoretical Frameworks

Privacy, in the context of virtual environments, can be understood through several theoretical lenses. One foundational theory is Westin's Privacy Framework, which categorizes privacy into four main dimensions: solitude, intimacy, anonymity, and reserve. In virtual environments, these dimensions manifest as follows:

- **Solitude:** Users often seek solitude in virtual spaces, desiring moments where they can engage without external observation.

- **Intimacy:** Users share personal experiences and emotions, leading to a need for secure channels of communication.

- **Anonymity:** Many virtual environments allow users to create avatars, leading to a complex relationship between identity and privacy.

- **Reserve:** Users may wish to control the flow of personal information, choosing what to disclose and to whom.

Furthermore, the concept of *contextual integrity*, proposed by Helen Nissenbaum, emphasizes that privacy is not merely about control over information but about the appropriateness of information flow in specific contexts. In virtual environments, the context often shifts rapidly, complicating users' ability to maintain privacy.

Challenges to Privacy in Virtual Environments

The challenges to ensuring privacy and data protection in VR are manifold:

1. **Data Collection and Surveillance:** VR platforms often collect extensive data on user interactions, preferences, and movements. This data can be used for targeted advertising or even surveillance, leading to a breach of user trust.

2. **Informed Consent:** Users may not fully understand the implications of their data sharing. The complexity of privacy policies often leads to uninformed consent, where users agree to terms without comprehending the extent of data usage.

3. **Data Breaches:** As with any digital platform, VR environments are susceptible to hacking and data breaches. These incidents can expose sensitive personal information, leading to identity theft and other malicious uses.

4. **Third-Party Access:** Many VR applications rely on third-party services for functionality, which can lead to unintended data sharing. Users may not be aware that their information is being accessed by external entities.

5. **Behavioral Tracking:** VR systems often track user behavior to enhance the immersive experience. However, this tracking can infringe on privacy if not transparently communicated and properly managed.

Examples of Privacy Violations

Several high-profile incidents have highlighted the critical need for robust privacy measures in virtual environments:

- **Facebook's Oculus:** The integration of Oculus into the Facebook ecosystem raised significant privacy concerns. Users were required to link their Oculus accounts to Facebook, leading to fears about data sharing between the two platforms. Reports indicated that Facebook used Oculus data to enhance user profiling for advertising purposes, raising ethical questions about informed consent and user autonomy.

- **Second Life:** In the virtual world of Second Life, users have reported instances of harassment and privacy violations, including the unauthorized sharing of personal information. The platform's reliance on user-generated content has made it challenging to enforce privacy measures effectively.

- **VR Chat:** VR Chat has faced scrutiny over issues of harassment and user safety. The platform's open nature allows for anonymity, but this can lead to abusive behavior, with users feeling unsafe due to the lack of effective moderation and privacy protections.

Best Practices for Ensuring Privacy

To address these challenges, several best practices can be implemented:

1. **Transparent Privacy Policies:** VR companies should adopt clear and accessible privacy policies that outline data collection practices, usage, and sharing. Users should be empowered to make informed choices regarding their data.

2. **User Control Over Data:** Platforms should enable users to control their data, including options to delete or modify personal information and to opt-out of data collection practices.

3. **Robust Security Measures:** Implementing strong cybersecurity protocols is essential to protect user data from breaches. This includes encryption, secure authentication processes, and regular security audits.

4. **Ethical Design Principles:** Developers should incorporate ethical design principles that prioritize user privacy from the outset, ensuring that privacy considerations are integrated into the development process.

5. **Community Guidelines and Moderation:** Establishing clear community guidelines and effective moderation systems can help create safer virtual environments, reducing the risk of harassment and privacy violations.

Conclusion

Ensuring privacy and data protection in virtual environments is a multifaceted challenge that requires a concerted effort from developers, policymakers, and users alike. By embracing transparency, user control, and ethical design practices, the VR industry can foster trust and create immersive experiences that respect user privacy. As we advance into an era where virtual realities become increasingly intertwined with our daily lives, prioritizing privacy will be paramount to ensuring that these spaces remain safe and welcoming for all users.

Bibliography

[1] Westin, A. F. (1967). *Privacy and Freedom*. New York: Atheneum.

[2] Nissenbaum, H. (2004). Privacy as Contextual Integrity. *Washington Law Review*, 79(1), 101-139.

[3] Oculus. (2019). *Oculus Privacy Policy*. Retrieved from `https://www.oculus.com/legal/privacy-policy/`

[4] Second Life. (2020). *Second Life Community Standards*. Retrieved from `https://community.secondlife.com/`

[5] VR Chat. (2021). *VRChat Community Guidelines*. Retrieved from `https://vrchat.com/home/guidelines`

Addressing Issues of Harassment and Discrimination in Virtual Reality

In recent years, the proliferation of virtual reality (VR) environments has raised significant concerns regarding harassment and discrimination. These issues not only undermine the immersive experience of VR but also reflect and amplify societal prejudices that exist in the physical world. This section explores the theoretical frameworks surrounding harassment and discrimination in virtual spaces, identifies prevalent problems, and discusses potential solutions through a cultural and ethical lens.

Theoretical Framework

To understand harassment and discrimination in VR, it is essential to consider the concept of *social presence*. Social presence refers to the degree to which a person feels they are in the company of others in a virtual environment. The higher the sense of social presence, the more likely individuals will experience real emotions and reactions to interactions, whether positive or negative. According to [?], social presence can significantly influence user behavior, leading to increased instances of harassment when individuals feel emboldened by anonymity.

Additionally, the *Online Disinhibition Effect* posits that individuals may act out in ways they would not in face-to-face interactions due to the perceived anonymity and distance provided by virtual environments [1]. This disinhibition can lead to aggressive behavior, including harassment and discriminatory remarks, as users feel less accountable for their actions.

Prevalent Problems

Harassment in VR can take various forms, including verbal abuse, unwanted sexual advances, and stalking. For instance, a 2020 study by [?] reported that 70% of female VR users experienced some form of harassment in virtual spaces. This alarming statistic highlights the urgent need for effective measures to combat such behavior.

Discrimination in VR often intersects with issues of race, gender, and sexuality. Users from marginalized backgrounds frequently report feeling unsafe or unwelcome in VR environments. For example, [?] documented instances where players of color were subjected to racial slurs and derogatory comments during gameplay. Such experiences not only detract from the enjoyment of VR but can also have lasting psychological effects on victims, leading to anxiety and a reluctance to engage in virtual experiences.

Case Studies

Several high-profile cases illustrate the severity of harassment and discrimination in VR. In 2016, a user reported being sexually harassed in the popular VR game *AltspaceVR*, where male avatars surrounded and groped her virtual representation. This incident sparked widespread discussions about the need for better reporting mechanisms and community guidelines to protect users from harassment.

Moreover, in 2018, the game *VRChat* faced backlash after numerous reports of users being targeted based on their race and gender. The developers responded by implementing stricter moderation policies and encouraging users to report harassment. However, the effectiveness of these measures remains a topic of debate, as many users argue that the reporting system is often inadequate.

Potential Solutions

Addressing harassment and discrimination in VR requires a multifaceted approach. First and foremost, developers must prioritize the implementation of robust reporting and moderation systems. This includes creating clear community guidelines that outline unacceptable behavior and establishing consequences for violators.

Education and awareness are also crucial in combating these issues. Users should be informed about the impact of their actions in virtual environments and encouraged to foster inclusive and respectful interactions. Training programs and workshops can help users understand the implications of harassment and discrimination, promoting a culture of empathy and respect.

Furthermore, incorporating ethical design principles into VR environments can help mitigate harassment. This includes features such as customizable privacy settings, where users can control who can interact with them, and safe zones where individuals can escape from harassment.

Conclusion

In conclusion, harassment and discrimination in virtual reality pose significant challenges that must be addressed to create safe and inclusive environments for all users. By understanding the theoretical underpinnings of these issues, recognizing prevalent problems, and implementing effective solutions, we can work towards a future where virtual reality is a space for positive and enriching interactions. As VR technology continues to evolve, it is imperative that ethical considerations remain at the forefront of its development, ensuring that all individuals can enjoy the benefits of virtual experiences without fear of harassment or discrimination.

Virtual Reality and Freedom of Speech

The advent of virtual reality (VR) has brought forth new dimensions to the concept of freedom of speech, a fundamental human right that allows individuals to express their opinions and ideas without fear of censorship or retaliation. In the realm of VR, this right faces unique challenges and opportunities, raising questions about the regulation of speech in immersive environments and the implications for users' rights.

Theoretical Framework

Freedom of speech is grounded in democratic principles that promote open discourse and the exchange of ideas. According to the *Universal Declaration of Human Rights* (UDHR), Article 19 states:

> Everyone has the right to freedom of opinion and expression; this right includes freedom to hold opinions without interference and to seek, receive and impart information and ideas through any media and regardless of frontiers.

In the context of VR, this principle must be examined through the lens of both *digital rights* and *immersive experiences*. Theories of communication, such as *Habermas's Public Sphere*, emphasize the importance of dialogue and participation in democratic societies, suggesting that VR can serve as a new public sphere where individuals engage in discourse. However, the immersive nature of VR complicates this dynamic, as users may experience heightened emotional responses and a sense of presence that can amplify the impact of speech—both positive and negative.

Challenges to Freedom of Speech in Virtual Reality

Despite the potential for VR to enhance freedom of speech, several challenges arise:

1. **Content Moderation:** Virtual worlds often employ content moderation policies to maintain community standards. While these policies are necessary to prevent hate speech and harassment, they can also lead to overreach, resulting in the suppression of legitimate expression. For example, platforms like *VRChat* have faced criticism for banning users based on vague guidelines, raising concerns about arbitrary censorship.

2. **Anonymity and Accountability:** The anonymity afforded by VR can embolden users to express themselves without fear of repercussions. However, this can also lead to the proliferation of harmful speech, including hate speech and cyberbullying. The challenge lies in balancing user anonymity with accountability, a dilemma that has prompted discussions around identity verification in virtual spaces.

3. **Platform Control:** Major VR platforms, such as *Oculus* and *SteamVR*, wield significant control over the content available to users. This corporate influence raises questions about who gets to decide what constitutes acceptable speech. For instance, if a platform decides to ban political

discourse, it effectively curtails users' freedom to engage in important conversations.

4. **Cultural Sensitivity:** VR environments are often global, bringing together users from diverse cultural backgrounds. What may be acceptable speech in one culture could be considered offensive in another. This cultural clash necessitates a nuanced approach to freedom of speech, where respect for cultural differences must be balanced against the right to express oneself.

Examples of Freedom of Speech Issues in Virtual Reality

Several notable incidents illustrate the complexities of freedom of speech within VR:

- **The *AltspaceVR* Incident:** In 2018, users of the social VR platform *AltspaceVR* organized a virtual event to discuss political issues. The platform's moderators intervened, citing concerns over hate speech. This incident sparked a debate about the limits of free expression in a moderated space, as users felt their right to discuss contentious topics was being infringed upon.

- **Virtual Protests:** Activists have utilized VR to stage protests and express dissent. For example, during the 2020 Black Lives Matter protests, some users created virtual demonstrations in VR spaces, highlighting social justice issues. However, these actions also led to platform backlash, with some VR environments banning such activities, raising questions about the right to protest in virtual settings.

- **Censorship in *Rec Room*:** In 2021, users in *Rec Room* reported instances of censorship where discussions about LGBTQ+ rights were moderated heavily. The platform's policies aimed to create a safe space but inadvertently silenced crucial conversations about identity and rights, demonstrating the delicate balance between safety and freedom.

Promoting Freedom of Speech in Virtual Reality

To foster an environment where freedom of speech thrives in VR, several strategies can be implemented:

1. **Transparent Moderation Policies:** VR platforms should adopt clear and transparent moderation policies that define acceptable speech while

protecting users' rights. Engaging users in the development of these policies can enhance trust and ensure that diverse perspectives are considered.

2. **Encouraging Dialogue:** Platforms can facilitate open dialogues about sensitive topics, allowing users to express differing viewpoints in a respectful manner. This approach can cultivate understanding and empathy among users, fostering a healthier discourse.

3. **User Empowerment:** Providing users with tools to manage their experiences, such as customizable filters for content they wish to avoid, empowers individuals to curate their interactions without infringing on others' rights to speak.

4. **Legal Frameworks:** Governments and international bodies must consider the implications of VR on freedom of speech, developing legal frameworks that protect users' rights while addressing the unique challenges posed by immersive technologies.

Conclusion

The intersection of virtual reality and freedom of speech presents a complex landscape that requires careful navigation. As VR continues to evolve, the principles of open expression must be upheld while addressing the challenges posed by moderation, anonymity, and cultural sensitivity. By fostering an environment that encourages dialogue and respects diverse perspectives, we can harness the potential of VR as a platform for meaningful expression and democratic engagement.

Bibliography

[1] United Nations. (1948). *Universal Declaration of Human Rights*.

[2] Habermas, J. (1962). *The Structural Transformation of the Public Sphere*.

[3] VRChat Inc. (n.d.). *Community Guidelines*.

[4] AltspaceVR. (2018). *Community Standards*.

[5] Rec Room Inc. (2021). *Code of Conduct*.

The Right to Disconnect in Virtual Reality

In an increasingly interconnected world, the concept of the "Right to Disconnect" has emerged as a critical issue, particularly in the context of virtual reality (VR). This right refers to the ability of individuals to disengage from digital environments without facing repercussions, whether socially, professionally, or psychologically. As VR technologies become more pervasive, understanding and advocating for this right is essential to ensure the well-being of users.

Theoretical Framework

The Right to Disconnect is grounded in several theoretical frameworks, including digital labor theory and the ethics of care. Digital labor theory examines the implications of constant connectivity on workers' rights and mental health. In VR, this theory extends to the immersive nature of the medium, where the boundaries between work and leisure can become blurred. The ethics of care emphasizes the importance of relationships and the well-being of individuals, asserting that technological environments must prioritize user health over productivity.

Problems Associated with the Right to Disconnect

1. **Increased Immersion and Engagement**: VR environments are designed to be immersive, often leading users to lose track of time and become overly engaged. This can result in prolonged usage without breaks, leading to physical and mental fatigue. Research indicates that extended exposure to VR can contribute to symptoms such as eye strain, headaches, and disorientation [1].

2. **Social Expectations and Peer Pressure**: In virtual communities, social norms can dictate participation levels. Users may feel pressured to remain online to maintain relationships, participate in events, or keep up with peers. This phenomenon can lead to a culture of constant availability, undermining the right to disconnect.

3. **Workplace Demands**: As VR technology is increasingly integrated into professional settings, employees may face expectations to remain connected outside of traditional working hours. This can lead to burnout and decreased job satisfaction, as employees struggle to separate their personal lives from work obligations.

4. **Lack of Regulation**: Currently, there are few regulations governing the right to disconnect in digital environments, including VR. This absence of legal frameworks can leave users vulnerable to exploitation and stress, as companies may prioritize productivity over employee well-being.

Examples of Disconnect Policies

Some organizations have begun to implement policies that support the Right to Disconnect. For instance, in 2017, France enacted a law that allows employees to ignore work emails outside of their designated hours without facing consequences. While this law does not explicitly cover VR environments, it sets a precedent for protecting workers' rights in the digital age.

Similarly, companies like Volkswagen have introduced a policy that disables emails sent to employees after hours. Such initiatives could be adapted for VR settings, creating protocols that encourage users to log off and take breaks, especially in immersive environments.

Ethical Considerations

From an ethical standpoint, the Right to Disconnect in VR raises several questions:
- **User Autonomy**: Users should have the autonomy to choose when to engage or disengage from VR environments. This autonomy is essential for fostering a healthy relationship with technology.

- **Responsibility of Developers**: VR developers and companies have a responsibility to create environments that respect users' rights to disconnect. This includes designing systems that remind users to take breaks and providing options to customize notifications and engagement levels.

- **Mental Health Implications**: The psychological impact of constant connectivity cannot be understated. VR experiences can be emotionally intense, and users need the opportunity to process these experiences without the pressure to remain connected.

Conclusion

The Right to Disconnect in virtual reality is a vital consideration in the ongoing development and integration of VR technologies. As we navigate the complexities of immersive environments, it is crucial to advocate for policies and practices that prioritize user well-being. By fostering a culture that respects the need for disconnection, we can create healthier virtual spaces that enhance rather than detract from the human experience.

Bibliography

[1] Smith, J. (2020). *The Effects of Extended Virtual Reality Use on User Health.* Journal of Virtual Environments, 12(3), 45-67.

Regulating Virtual Reality Technologies: A Human Rights Perspective

The rapid development of virtual reality (VR) technologies has transformed the way individuals interact with digital environments, raising significant ethical and human rights concerns. As VR continues to permeate various aspects of daily life, it is imperative to examine how regulatory frameworks can be established to safeguard human rights within these immersive spaces.

The Need for Regulation

Regulation of VR technologies is essential due to several factors:

- **User Privacy:** With the extensive data collected from users, including biometric information, location tracking, and behavioral patterns, the potential for misuse is substantial. The General Data Protection Regulation (GDPR) in the European Union serves as a model for protecting user data, but its applicability to VR remains unclear.

- **Content Moderation:** VR environments can harbor harmful content, including hate speech, harassment, and violence. Establishing guidelines for content moderation is crucial to create safe virtual spaces, akin to regulations imposed on social media platforms.

- **Accessibility:** Ensuring that VR technologies are accessible to all, including individuals with disabilities, is a fundamental human right. Regulation can mandate that VR developers adhere to accessibility standards, similar to those required in physical spaces.

Theoretical Frameworks for Regulation

To approach the regulation of VR technologies from a human rights perspective, several theoretical frameworks can be applied:

- **The Capability Approach:** Proposed by Amartya Sen and Martha Nussbaum, this framework emphasizes the importance of enabling individuals to achieve their full potential. In the context of VR, this means ensuring that technologies do not limit users' capabilities but rather enhance their experiences and opportunities.

- **The Social Contract Theory:** This theory posits that individuals consent to form a society and abide by its rules for mutual benefit. Applying this to VR suggests that developers and users enter a social contract where developers must ensure ethical practices and protect user rights.

Challenges in Regulation

Regulating VR technologies presents several challenges:

- **Rapid Technological Advancements:** The pace of innovation in VR often outstrips existing regulatory frameworks, leading to a reactive rather than proactive approach to regulation. Policymakers must stay ahead of technological trends to effectively protect human rights.

- **Global Disparities:** Different countries have varying standards for human rights and technology regulation. This disparity complicates the establishment of a unified regulatory framework for global VR platforms, as developers must navigate a patchwork of laws.

- **Industry Resistance:** The VR industry may resist regulation, arguing that it stifles innovation. Striking a balance between fostering innovation and protecting human rights is crucial.

Examples of Regulatory Approaches

Several countries and organizations are beginning to address the regulation of VR technologies:

- **European Union:** The EU has proposed regulations that specifically address digital services, including VR platforms. The Digital Services Act aims to create safer online spaces by imposing stricter content moderation and transparency requirements on tech companies.

- **United States:** In the U.S., the Federal Trade Commission (FTC) has started to investigate VR companies for potential violations of consumer protection laws, particularly concerning privacy and data security.

- **International Organizations:** The United Nations has recognized the need for guidelines on digital technologies, including VR, to ensure they align with human rights standards. Initiatives such as the UN Guiding Principles on Business and Human Rights provide a framework for companies to assess their impact on human rights.

Conclusion

The regulation of virtual reality technologies from a human rights perspective is not just a theoretical exercise; it is a pressing necessity as VR becomes more integrated into society. By establishing comprehensive regulatory frameworks that prioritize user privacy, accessibility, and content moderation, we can create a virtual landscape that respects and promotes human rights. The challenge lies in crafting regulations that are flexible enough to adapt to rapid technological changes while robust enough to protect individuals in these immersive environments. It is imperative for stakeholders—governments, developers, and users—to collaborate in shaping a future where virtual reality enhances human experiences without compromising fundamental rights.

$$\text{Human Rights} \to \text{Regulation} \to \text{Virtual Reality} \qquad (12)$$

Ethical Considerations in Promoting Inclusivity and Diversity in Virtual Reality

In the rapidly evolving landscape of virtual reality (VR), the promotion of inclusivity and diversity has become a critical ethical consideration. As virtual environments increasingly reflect and influence real-world interactions, it is imperative to understand the implications of these digital spaces on marginalized communities. This section explores the ethical frameworks necessary for fostering inclusivity and diversity in VR, the challenges faced, and practical examples of successful initiatives.

Theoretical Frameworks

To navigate the ethical landscape of inclusivity in VR, several theoretical frameworks can be applied. One prominent theory is **Social Justice Theory**, which emphasizes the fair distribution of resources and opportunities across all societal groups. In the context of VR, this theory advocates for equal access to virtual spaces and the representation of diverse identities. Another relevant framework is **Critical Race Theory**, which interrogates the intersections of race, technology, and power. This theory can guide developers and stakeholders in recognizing and dismantling systemic biases that may be perpetuated in virtual environments.

Challenges to Inclusivity and Diversity

Despite the potential of VR to serve as a platform for inclusivity, several challenges hinder progress:

1. **Access Barriers:** The digital divide remains a significant obstacle. Socioeconomic disparities can limit access to VR technologies, thereby excluding low-income individuals and communities from participation. A study by Pew Research Center (2021) highlights that 23% of Americans with household incomes below $30,000 lack access to high-speed internet, which is essential for immersive VR experiences.

2. **Representation Issues:** Many VR experiences fail to accurately represent diverse cultures, identities, and narratives. This lack of representation can alienate users who do not see themselves reflected in the virtual world. For instance, the gaming industry has faced criticism for its historically narrow portrayal of characters, often sidelining women and people of color.

3. **Harassment and Discrimination:** Virtual environments can become breeding grounds for harassment and discrimination. A report by the Anti-Defamation League (2020) revealed that 53% of gamers have experienced harassment while playing online. This toxicity can discourage marginalized groups from engaging in virtual spaces, thereby perpetuating a cycle of exclusion.

4. **Cultural Appropriation:** The appropriation of cultural elements without proper context or respect can lead to misunderstandings and reinforce stereotypes. For example, the use of Indigenous symbols in VR games without consultation or consent from Indigenous communities raises ethical concerns about representation and ownership.

Promoting Inclusivity and Diversity: Best Practices

To address these challenges, developers, researchers, and policymakers must adopt best practices that promote inclusivity and diversity in VR:

1. **User-Centered Design:** Implementing a user-centered design approach ensures that diverse voices are included in the development process. Engaging with community members during the design phase can lead to more authentic and representative virtual experiences. For instance, the game *Spiritfarer* features a diverse cast of characters and was developed with input from cultural consultants to ensure respectful representation.

2. **Accessibility Features:** Integrating accessibility features, such as customizable controls and visual/audio aids, can make VR experiences more inclusive for individuals with disabilities. The game *Beat Saber* has incorporated accessibility options that allow players with varying abilities to enjoy the game, demonstrating a commitment to inclusivity.

3. **Education and Awareness:** Raising awareness about the importance of diversity in VR can foster a more inclusive culture within the industry. Workshops, seminars, and educational campaigns can equip developers with the knowledge necessary to create respectful and representative content.

4. **Community Guidelines:** Establishing clear community guidelines that promote respectful behavior and inclusivity can help mitigate harassment and discrimination. Platforms like *VRChat* have implemented codes of conduct that encourage positive interactions among users, fostering a more welcoming environment.

Case Studies

Several initiatives exemplify successful efforts to promote inclusivity and diversity in VR:

- **Project ARA:** This initiative focuses on creating a VR platform that centers on the experiences of marginalized communities. By prioritizing user input from diverse backgrounds, Project ARA aims to create virtual spaces that reflect a wide range of identities and narratives.

- **The Virtual Reality Diversity Initiative (VRDI):** Established to support underrepresented creators in the VR space, VRDI provides resources, mentorship, and funding to individuals from diverse backgrounds. This initiative not only empowers creators but also enriches the VR landscape with varied perspectives.

Conclusion

Promoting inclusivity and diversity in virtual reality is not merely an ethical obligation; it is essential for the evolution of immersive technologies that reflect the richness of human experience. By addressing access barriers, representation issues, and fostering respectful interactions, the VR community can create spaces that are not only technologically advanced but also socially responsible. As we move forward, it is crucial to remain vigilant and committed to ethical practices that uplift all voices in the virtual realm, ensuring that no one is left behind in the digital age.

$$\text{Inclusivity Index} = \frac{\text{Number of Represented Identities}}{\text{Total Possible Identities}} \times 100 \quad (13)$$

The Inclusivity Index serves as a quantitative measure of diversity within a virtual environment, guiding developers in their efforts to create more inclusive spaces.

The Future of Virtual Reality and Human Rights

The rapid advancement of virtual reality (VR) technology presents both unprecedented opportunities and significant challenges in the realm of human rights. As VR becomes increasingly integrated into everyday life, it is crucial to assess its implications for fundamental rights, ensuring that the digital landscape remains inclusive, equitable, and respectful of individual freedoms.

Emerging Technologies and Human Rights

The future of VR is closely tied to the evolution of emerging technologies, such as artificial intelligence (AI), machine learning, and blockchain. These technologies can enhance the VR experience but also raise ethical concerns. For instance, AI-driven algorithms can personalize content in ways that may inadvertently reinforce biases or exclude marginalized groups. The challenge lies in developing AI systems that promote fairness and inclusivity while respecting users' rights to privacy and data protection.

Accessibility and Inclusion

One of the most pressing issues in the future of VR is ensuring accessibility for all users, particularly those with disabilities. Current VR technologies often fail to accommodate various physical and cognitive impairments, leading to a digital divide that exacerbates existing inequalities. To address this, developers must prioritize inclusive design principles, creating VR environments that are navigable and usable by individuals with diverse needs. This includes implementing features such as voice commands, haptic feedback, and customizable interfaces.

Privacy and Data Protection

As users engage with VR platforms, they generate vast amounts of personal data, raising concerns about privacy and data security. The collection, storage, and use of sensitive information must adhere to strict ethical guidelines and legal frameworks. The General Data Protection Regulation (GDPR) in the European Union serves as a model for protecting user data, but compliance can be challenging in the rapidly evolving VR landscape. Future regulations should focus on transparency, user consent, and the right to be forgotten, ensuring that individuals retain control over their personal information.

Freedom of Expression and Censorship

The immersive nature of VR can amplify both the benefits and risks associated with freedom of expression. On one hand, VR can serve as a powerful tool for social change, enabling users to experience diverse perspectives and engage in meaningful dialogue. On the other hand, there is a risk of censorship, particularly in authoritarian regimes where governments may seek to control VR content. The future of VR must prioritize the protection of free speech while also addressing the potential for hate speech and harmful content. Establishing clear guidelines for content moderation that respect human rights is essential.

Combating Harassment and Discrimination

As virtual environments become social spaces, the potential for harassment and discrimination increases. Users may face abuse based on their identity, leading to a hostile environment that undermines their rights. Developers and platform providers must implement robust anti-harassment policies and tools to protect users from abuse. This includes reporting mechanisms, community guidelines, and educational initiatives to foster a culture of respect and empathy within virtual communities.

Global Perspectives and Cultural Sensitivity

The global nature of VR presents unique challenges in addressing human rights. Cultural differences can influence perceptions of rights and responsibilities, necessitating a nuanced approach to VR development. Stakeholders must engage with diverse communities to understand their values and concerns, ensuring that VR technologies are culturally sensitive and promote inclusivity. This engagement can help prevent cultural appropriation and ensure that indigenous knowledge and rights are respected in virtual spaces.

The Role of Stakeholders

The future of VR and human rights will depend on the collaboration of various stakeholders, including technologists, policymakers, civil society organizations, and users. A multi-stakeholder approach can foster dialogue and collaboration, leading to the development of ethical frameworks that prioritize human rights in VR design and implementation. Initiatives such as the Virtual Reality Developers Association (VRDA) can play a pivotal role in promoting best practices and advocating for users' rights.

Conclusion

In conclusion, the future of virtual reality holds immense potential for enhancing human rights, but it also presents significant challenges that must be addressed proactively. By prioritizing accessibility, privacy, freedom of expression, and cultural sensitivity, stakeholders can harness the transformative power of VR to create inclusive and equitable digital spaces. As we navigate this evolving landscape, it is imperative to remain vigilant and committed to upholding the principles of human dignity and respect for all individuals in the virtual realm.

$$R_{VR} = f(A, P, C, E) \qquad (14)$$

where R_{VR} represents the overall respect for human rights in virtual reality, A is accessibility, P is privacy, C is cultural sensitivity, and E is the empowerment of users through education and engagement.

This equation illustrates that the respect for human rights in virtual reality is a function of multiple interdependent factors. Ensuring a balanced approach to these elements will be critical in shaping a future where virtual reality serves as a tool for promoting, rather than undermining, human rights.

Index

ability, 26, 30, 36, 91, 96, 97, 105
abuse, 9, 127
acceptance, 17, 40
access, 2, 93, 97, 100, 101, 105, 106, 126
accessibility, 2, 4, 93, 100, 102–104, 126, 128
accountability, 36, 59, 60
acknowledgment, 70
acquisition, 92
act, 59
adaptation, 102
addiction, 2, 4
adoption, 4, 105, 106
advance, 109
advantage, 31
advent, 4
adventure, 39
advertising, 25
advocacy, 92
advocate, 70, 119
afterthought, 25
age, 31, 37, 118, 126
agency, 63
aggregation, 25
alienation, 70
AltspaceVR, 37
amount, 24

anonymity, 25, 31, 36, 59, 79, 107, 116
anxiety, 14, 30, 34, 62
appearance, 17, 33
application, 46
appreciation, 92
approach, 11, 25, 34, 50, 98, 101, 113, 122, 128
appropriation, 9, 14, 70, 78, 84–86, 128
arcade, 4
area, 11
assignment, 45
atmosphere, 31
attack, 78
attention, 4, 103
attire, 70
attribute, 102
authenticity, 14, 15, 23, 25, 30, 32, 40
author, 1
autonomy, 14
availability, 93
avatar, 8, 13, 14, 16–18, 23, 25, 30–33, 36, 37, 39
awareness, 86, 92, 105, 113

back, 1

background, 16, 101
backlash, 78
balancing, 36, 37, 39, 62
barrier, 93, 97, 106
base, 42
beauty, 33, 39
behavior, 8, 17, 20, 25, 30, 31, 37, 42, 46, 57, 58, 60, 63–65, 113
being, 5, 25, 31, 32, 34, 40, 53, 71, 117, 119
belonging, 17, 37
benefit, 2, 97, 101
bias, 91
blur, 57
body, 18, 27, 28, 31, 33, 36
book, 8
break, 88
bridging, 93, 107
budget, 105
building, 93
bullying, 34
burden, 45

campaign, 4
capability, 4
care, 117
case, 11, 25, 39, 62
cast, 78
censor, 25
censorship, 127
challenge, 25, 37, 58, 70, 109
change, 8, 20, 127
character, 39
choice, 14
class, 70
clothing, 97
collaboration, 71, 84, 93
collection, 14, 24

combination, 11
comfort, 4
commitment, 32, 36, 96
commodification, 70, 96
communication, 79, 82–84, 91
community, 9, 37, 46, 55, 65, 71, 78, 113, 126, 127
compassion, 33, 50, 92
complexity, 63
compliance, 60
computer, 1, 3
concept, 15, 37, 40, 46, 56, 96
concern, 57
conclusion, 5, 9, 12, 18, 34, 43, 45, 48, 50, 58, 60, 62, 71, 86, 93, 96, 101, 103, 113, 128
confidence, 30, 34
conflict, 53, 78, 79
confusion, 29, 57
connectivity, 117
consciousness, 2
consent, 5, 8, 25, 32, 46, 96, 97
consequence, 102
consideration, 5, 53, 60, 71, 86, 119
console, 4
construct, 92
constructivism, 35
content, 14, 20, 37, 53, 93, 106, 127
context, 59, 70, 78, 93, 97, 107
contract, 45, 46
contrast, 105
control, 96, 98, 109, 113, 127
creation, 20, 25, 32, 97, 102
creativity, 26, 37
creature, 31
criticism, 78
culture, 25, 60, 65, 70, 78, 113, 119, 127
curation, 14

Index

customization, 13, 18
cutting, 105
cyberbullying, 25, 36
cycle, 31, 100, 105

data, 5, 14, 24, 25, 36, 108, 109
date, 1
deception, 30, 32
decline, 4
defamation, 25
degree, 91
depression, 30, 34
desensitization, 50
design, 1, 3, 8, 9, 17, 25, 26, 34, 36, 55, 58, 61, 62, 70, 96, 105, 109, 113, 127
desire, 15, 62
detachment, 33, 57
determination, 96
developer, 78
development, 2–4, 8, 26, 34, 43, 50, 58, 71, 93, 97, 98, 100, 102, 113, 119, 128
dialogue, 7, 37, 60, 84, 93, 116, 127
dichotomy, 59
dignity, 18, 128
dilemma, 36, 37
direction, 53
disability, 102
disassociation, 60
discomfort, 93
disconnect, 4, 30
disconnection, 33, 45, 119
discourse, 24, 35, 60, 62, 78
discrimination, 17, 31, 46, 113, 127
discussion, 4, 50, 71
disengagement, 50, 59
disinhibition, 36
disparity, 39, 105

display, 4
dissociation, 34
dissonance, 14, 23, 29
distinction, 2, 37
distress, 33, 93
distribution, 101
diversity, 70, 72, 92, 96, 100, 125, 126
divide, 97, 99–101, 105, 106, 127
door, 25

edge, 105
education, 2, 5, 100, 105
effect, 33
effectiveness, 60, 93
effort, 40, 109
emergence, 4, 43
empathy, 33, 34, 37, 49, 50, 63, 65, 74, 84, 88, 91, 93, 113, 127
endeavor, 79
enforcement, 60
engagement, 7, 8, 15, 20, 26, 71, 106, 116, 128
engineering, 105
enjoyment, 78
entertainment, 2, 4, 6
environment, 1, 4, 5, 8, 9, 16–18, 33, 53, 79, 115, 116, 126, 127
equation, 8, 16, 40, 59, 60, 63, 128
equilibrium, 40
equity, 2, 97, 106
era, 109
escapism, 4
establishment, 60
estate, 5
ethnicity, 70
evolution, 4, 5, 47, 126
examination, 37, 58

example, 14, 31, 33, 36, 39, 62, 70, 78, 101, 106
exchange, 46, 70, 86, 88, 89, 93
excitement, 4
existence, 2, 37, 60
experience, 1, 2, 8–10, 23, 25, 26, 29, 30, 33, 36, 40, 55, 62, 74, 78, 91, 105, 106, 119, 126, 127
experiment, 2
exploitation, 14, 30, 36, 86, 97, 98
exploration, 14, 29–34, 37, 43
exposure, 105
expression, 14, 17, 18, 31, 32, 35–37, 70, 97, 114, 116, 127, 128
extent, 102

face, 17, 106, 127
faction, 13
failure, 4
familiarity, 105
fantasy, 57
fear, 25, 59, 62, 113
feature, 97
feedback, 78, 127
feeling, 33
fiction, 2
field, 63
film, 2, 8
focus, 20
following, 11, 31, 47
force, 93
forefront, 113
foster, 9, 10, 26, 32, 33, 53, 64, 65, 74, 79, 88, 92, 93, 109, 113, 115, 127
foundation, 42
fragmentation, 14, 29

framework, 9, 60
France, 118
freedom, 18, 78, 114–116, 127, 128
frontier, 9
function, 8, 128
funding, 4
future, 5, 43, 47, 60, 65, 107, 113, 126–128

game, 13, 25, 78
gaming, 4, 25, 39, 70, 105
gap, 14, 105
gender, 31, 33, 36, 70
generation, 4
goal, 53
groundwork, 4
group, 13, 29

hand, 4, 46, 102, 127
haptic, 127
harassment, 5, 9, 17, 25, 30–32, 34, 36, 37, 45, 113, 127
harm, 50–53, 62
hate, 37, 127
head, 4
headset, 4
health, 2, 15, 34, 36, 40, 117
healthcare, 2, 5
Heilig, 1
heritage, 75, 76, 96, 97
highlight, 28, 52
homogenization, 100
human, 2, 5, 10, 11, 45, 70, 119, 122, 126–128
humanity, 3

identification, 30
identity, 2, 5, 11, 13–15, 23, 25, 29–35, 39, 40, 78, 96, 127
illusion, 1, 23

Index

image, 18, 27, 28, 31, 33, 36, 39
immersion, 8, 54, 63
impact, 2, 3, 7, 12, 23, 28, 30, 34, 37, 54, 55, 57, 58, 71, 73, 74, 93, 106, 113
implementation, 50, 60, 94, 113
importance, 1, 37, 84, 92, 94, 96, 117
impunity, 60
in, 1–5, 7, 9, 11, 13–15, 17, 18, 20, 23–27, 29–37, 39–43, 45, 46, 48, 50–55, 57–60, 62–65, 69–76, 78, 79, 82–86, 88, 91–94, 96–98, 101–109, 113, 115, 117–119, 125–128
inadequacy, 31
inclusion, 2
inclusivity, 37, 71, 72, 74, 89, 124–126, 128
increase, 20, 30, 59
indigenous, 128
individual, 18, 25, 32, 36, 39, 40, 102
industry, 6, 109
inequality, 105
infancy, 4, 43
influence, 13, 17, 20, 30, 56–58, 128
influencer, 39
information, 8, 14, 36, 97, 114
innovation, 4, 5, 7, 26
instance, 2, 5, 8, 13, 14, 25, 30, 31, 33, 34, 36, 78, 92, 97, 118
integration, 25, 119
integrity, 32
interaction, 91
interactionism, 29, 30, 35
interconnectedness, 37
interest, 3, 4
interference, 96, 114

interplay, 5, 12, 15, 20, 23, 40, 54, 59
intersection, 116
intimacy, 107
introduction, 4, 7
inventor, 1
issue, 30, 58, 71, 74, 98, 103

Jaron Lanier, 1
journey, 3
jurisdiction, 60

knowledge, 20, 92, 96–98, 105, 128

labor, 117
lack, 70, 97, 100, 105, 106
landscape, 10, 12, 40, 45, 48, 60, 96, 106, 107, 116, 128
language, 92
latency, 4
law, 45–48, 60, 118
learning, 20, 43, 48, 50, 71, 91–93, 101
leisure, 117
lens, 24
level, 8
leverage, 92
leveraging, 5, 65, 88, 93
life, 2, 14, 20, 30, 31, 33, 36–40, 53, 56–58, 84
limit, 93, 105
line, 39
literature, 2

manipulation, 14, 15, 25, 29–32, 62
manner, 92
material, 33
measure, 126
medium, 26, 63, 117
misappropriation, 97, 98
misrepresentation, 9, 14, 25, 30

mistrust, 25
misunderstanding, 93
misuse, 36
mitigation, 53
mobile, 4
moderation, 37, 113, 116, 127
moment, 4
morality, 5, 11, 55–58, 60
Morton Heilig, 1
motion, 4
motivation, 20
multiplayer, 13, 31, 78
multiplicity, 29

narrative, 62, 63
nature, 2, 8, 25, 30, 36, 45, 57, 59, 88, 117, 127, 128
navigation, 116
need, 9, 25, 34, 36, 60, 70, 78, 102, 108, 119
Nick Bostrom, 2
notion, 2, 23, 45

obligation, 126
occupation, 105
one, 1, 6, 30, 33, 40, 53, 96, 104, 126, 127
opinion, 114
opportunity, 101, 105
other, 4, 46, 70, 91, 102, 127
outline, 113
outset, 25, 102
oversimplification, 93

participation, 102
party, 25
people, 25, 102, 103
perception, 30, 34
performance, 20
period, 4

person, 14, 30, 91, 92
persona, 14, 15, 39
perspective, 33, 45, 53, 70, 92, 102, 122
phenomenon, 10, 15, 25, 30, 37, 39
Philip K. Dick's, 2
philosopher, 2
place, 33
platform, 25, 32, 33, 36, 37, 70, 92, 107, 116, 124, 127
play, 18, 69
player, 13, 39, 55, 78
playing, 39
policy, 58, 118
portrayal, 78
positivism, 45
potential, 2, 4, 5, 9, 14, 15, 20, 25, 30–33, 36, 45, 49, 51, 53, 55, 57, 58, 62, 70, 71, 74, 76, 82, 88, 91, 93, 97, 101, 105, 106, 114, 116, 124, 127, 128
power, 32, 69, 128
practice, 5
precedent, 118
presence, 8, 23, 60, 91, 93
presentation, 13
preservation, 75, 76
pressure, 15, 39
prevalence, 17
principle, 1, 25, 102
priority, 104
privacy, 5, 14, 15, 24–26, 36, 37, 46, 107–109, 113, 128
process, 9, 25, 40, 71, 93
productivity, 117
profile, 85, 108
profit, 97
progress, 124

Index

project, 4
promise, 50
promotion, 63
property, 96
protection, 25, 46, 96, 97, 108, 109, 127
public, 2, 4, 58
purpose, 10

quality, 91
quest, 3
question, 45, 55

race, 69, 70
range, 11
real, 2, 5, 14, 20, 23, 25, 29–31, 33, 34, 36–40, 45, 53, 56–58, 60, 78
reality, 1–3, 5, 7–12, 18, 20, 23, 26, 29, 31–34, 37, 43, 45, 55, 57, 59, 60, 62, 63, 65, 74, 79, 84, 88, 93, 96–98, 102–104, 107, 113, 116, 119, 126, 128
realm, 53, 126, 128
reflection, 40, 55, 63, 107
regulation, 32, 122
reinforcement, 31
relation, 45
relationship, 17, 40, 63
report, 9
reporting, 32, 113, 127
representation, 9, 14, 18, 23, 36, 37, 62, 69–71, 78, 86, 97, 98, 100, 106, 126
research, 7, 11, 20, 34, 58
reserve, 107
resistance, 106
resolution, 4, 79

respect, 9, 65, 71, 72, 78, 86, 96, 98, 109, 113, 127, 128
response, 37, 43
responsibility, 17, 32, 36, 45, 58, 59, 62, 86
result, 30, 31, 70, 97
resurgence, 4
richness, 70, 100, 126
right, 8, 36, 96, 97, 114
rise, 4
risk, 5, 9, 25, 62, 70, 97, 127
role, 18, 30, 39, 48, 70, 79, 93, 105

safeguarding, 32
safety, 31
salience, 91
scientist, 1
scope, 11
screen, 30
section, 11, 37, 50
self, 13, 14, 16, 25, 29–32, 34–37, 40, 96
sense, 8, 13, 14, 17, 25, 29–31, 34, 37, 57, 59, 70, 91
sensitivity, 9, 74, 93, 94, 96, 116, 128
Sensorama, 1
set, 15
sex, 33
shape, 12, 58, 70, 74
share, 14, 36, 97
sickness, 4
significance, 70, 78, 97
skepticism, 106
society, 2, 3, 7, 9, 12, 101
solitude, 107
sound, 1
sovereignty, 96, 98
space, 23, 30, 31, 37, 46, 55, 113
speech, 37, 114–116, 127

standpoint, 118
status, 100
stereotyping, 78
storytelling, 62, 63
stress, 39
struggle, 30, 39, 57, 105
study, 10–12, 69
success, 26, 39
summary, 3, 23
support, 48, 93, 118
surge, 3
surrounding, 2, 5, 14, 18
surveillance, 14, 25
sword, 31, 32

talk, 31
tapestry, 3, 31, 54
team, 78
teammate, 78
tech, 105
technology, 2, 4–7, 9, 10, 15, 23, 26, 34, 37, 45, 55, 60, 93, 97, 100, 101, 104–106, 113
tension, 59
term, 1, 20
the Oculus Rift, 4
theft, 25
theory, 13, 29, 30, 35, 45, 46, 50, 69, 70, 91, 92, 107, 117
thought, 2
time, 33
today, 1
toll, 39
tool, 50, 84, 93, 101, 127, 128
track, 14, 25
tracking, 4
training, 2, 5

transformation, 7
transparency, 8, 109
trivialization, 70
trust, 26, 30, 31, 109
type, 105

understanding, 10, 12, 20, 23, 26, 33, 37, 46, 50, 53, 55, 60, 62, 70, 71, 74, 78, 79, 84, 86, 88, 91–93, 96, 105, 107, 113
use, 2, 4, 5, 7, 15, 43, 70, 97
user, 1, 2, 4, 8, 14, 16, 17, 24–26, 30, 31, 33, 36, 37, 42, 45, 46, 60, 62, 63, 74, 109, 117, 119

validation, 15
verification, 25
view, 78, 106
violence, 50–53
virtuality, 2, 60
voice, 127

wage, 105
warrant, 43
warrior, 31
way, 33, 48, 53
well, 31, 32, 34, 40, 70, 117, 119
whole, 3, 12
willingness, 33
winter, 4
work, 1, 37, 60, 72, 74, 86, 105, 107, 113, 117, 118
workplace, 105
world, 5, 14, 20, 29, 30, 33, 34, 39, 45, 58, 60, 78, 84, 89, 93